KT-555-818

GUNG HO!

Other titles in this series

THE ONE MINUTE MANAGER
Ken Blanchard and Spencer Johnson

PUTTING THE ONE MINUTE MANAGER TO WORK
Ken Blanchard and Robert Lorber

THE ONE MINUTE SALES PERSON
Spencer Johnson

LEADERSHIP AND THE ONE MINUTE MANAGER
Ken Blanchard, Patricia Zigarmi and Drea Zigarmi

THE ONE MINUTE MANAGER MEETS THE MONKEY
Ken Blanchard, William Oncken Jr. and Hal Burrows

THE ONE MINUTE MANAGER BUILDS HIGH PERFORMING TEAMS
Ken Blanchard, Donald Carew and Eunice Parisi-Carew

RAVING FANS!
Ken Blanchard and Sheldon Bowles

BIG BUCKS!
Ken Blanchard and Sheldon Bowles

HIGH FIVE!
*Ken Blanchard, Sheldon Bowles, Don Carew
and Eunice Parisi-Carew*

LEADERSHIP BY THE BOOK
Ken Blanchard, Bill Hybels and Phil Hodges

THE LITTLE BOOK OF COACHING
Ken Blanchard and Don Shula

THE ONE MINUTE APOLOGY
Ken Blanchard and Margret McBride

THE ON-TIME, ON-TARGET MANAGER
Ken Blanchard and Steve Gottry

THE ONE MINUTE GOLFER
Ken Blanchard

KEN BLANCHARD
AND SHELDON BOWLES

GUNG HO!

HOW TO MOTIVATE PEOPLE IN ANY ORGANIZATION

HarperCollins*Publishers*

HarperCollins*Publishers*
77–85 Fulham Palace Road,
Hammersmith, London W6 8JB

www.harpercollins.co.uk

First published in the UK by Collins 1998
This edition published 2011

1

© The Blanchard Family Partnership Ode to Joy Limited 1998

'Stopping by Woods on a Snowy Evening' from
The Poetry of Robert Frost, edited by Edward Connery Lathem
© 1951 by Robert Frost, copyright 1923,
© 1969 by Henry Holt and Company, Inc.

The authors assert the moral right to be identified as the authors of this work

ISBN-978-0-00-653068-8

Printed and bound in Great Britain by Clays Ltd, St Ives plc

All rights reserved. No part of this publication may be reproduced,
stored in a retrieval system, or transmitted, in any form or by any
means, electronic, mechanical, photocopying, recording or otherwise,
without the prior permission of the publishers.

MIX
Paper from
responsible sources
FSC® C007454

FSC is a non-profit international organisation established to promote the
responsible management of the world's forests. Products carrying the FSC
label are independently certified to assure consumers that they come
from forests that are managed to meet the social, economic and
ecological needs of present and future generations.

Find out more about HarperCollins and the environment at
www.harpercollins.co.uk/green

Dedicated to the memory of

ANDREW CHARLES LONGCLAW
1940–1994
AND
HIS BELOVED WIFE, JEAN,
AND SON, ROBERT,

TRAGICALLY KILLED
September 1965

CONTENTS

FOREWORD   2

PROLOGUE   6

INTRODUCTION   11

THE GUNG HO STORY   15

AFTERWORD   132

GUNG HO GAME PLAN   135
    REASSESSMENT GUIDEPOST I   137
    REASSESSMENT GUIDEPOST II   138
    REASSESSMENT GUIDEPOST III   139

GOOSE HONKINGS   141

ABOUT THE AUTHORS   148

SERVICES AVAILABLE   151

SOCIAL NETWORKING   153

FOREWORD

by Ken Blanchard

The success of *The One Minute Manager* still amazes me. I was a college professor for ten years and had written a couple of textbooks, but never anything popular. I met the book's co-author, Spencer Johnson, at a cocktail party for authors in San Diego. Spencer had written a successful series of children's books called *Value Tales*. At the time we met he was working on a *One Minute Parent* book dealing with goal setting and feedback. I'd been teaching similar concepts, so invited Spencer to a seminar I was doing the following Monday. He sat in the back of the room, smiling and laughing. When it was over, he came running up and said, "Forget my parenting book. Let's do *The One Minute Manager*." I had been a storyteller as a professor and Spencer was a storyteller as a writer, so our idea was to write a parable around a few simple management secrets. That simplicity was, I think, the key to the popularity of *The One Minute Manager*. Based on its success, I started writing fun parables that told simple secrets to help people make work better.

Leadership and the One Minute Manager was one of the next books in the series. In the guise of a parable about the One Minute Manager, my coauthors Drea Zigarmi, Pat Zigarmi, and I taught the art of Situational Leadership® II, a concept I began developing with Paul Hersey in the 1960s. The book shows managers how to acquire and use the powerful skill of matching leadership style to the person and task at hand.

Then I was fortunate enough to meet Sheldon Bowles, one of the founders of a full-service gasoline chain in Western Canada called Domo Gas. Back in the 1970s, when everybody was going to self-service gasoline stations, Sheldon created stations that treated customers as though they were driving into a racecar pit stop. When a customer drove up, two or three people in red jumpsuits would run toward their car. As quickly as possible, they would look under the hood, clean the windshield, and pump the gas. Some stations would even give customers a cup of coffee and a newspaper, ask them to step out of the car, and dust-bust the interior. As customers pulled away, they would be given a flyer that said: "P.S. We also sell gas." The Domo Gas stations were a huge success.

Sheldon came to me and said, "Ken, I have a book I'd love to write with you." Since he knew all about creating satisfied customers, together we wrote *Raving Fans!: A Revolutionary Approach to Customer Service.* The book became an international bestseller.

After the successful publication of *Raving Fans!*, Sheldon and I realized that you can't create Raving Fan customers if your people are unmotivated and uncommitted. That led us to write *Gung Ho!*, an inspirational story of how to energize and empower your people. When the people who work with you are excited about your organization and what they're doing, they go out of their way to create Raving Fans.

The One Minute Manager Meets the Monkey is probably the most humorous book I've ever written, because Bill Oncken was one of the funniest guys I ever met. He was also a Princeton graduate and a great observer of people. When he was on the speakers' circuit, Bill often told his story about the monkey—you know, the one that shows up when somebody comes into your office and says, "Boss, we have a problem." Bill would always say, "Watch out, because the monkey's about to leap from their back onto yours." Monkeys have to be either shot or fed. If you take somebody else's monkey, you're in charge of its care and feeding. And whoever gave it to you will be in your office the next day saying, "I left that monkey with you. How are you doing with it?" Now you're doing their job. I loved this story so much that I went to Bill and said, "We've got to write a fun, simple book around this." Coauthored with Bill and one of his top trainers, Hal Burrows, *The One Minute Manager Meets the Monkey* became one of the most popular books in the series.

I'm really excited that these books are being reissued, because together they offer a powerful way to learn about being a manager. In fact, they could be an orientation program for all new managers. *The One Minute Manager* covers the basic principles of effective management. If you want to know how to bring out the best in people, then *Leadership and the One Minute Manager* is a trusted guide. But why is effective management important? Because you want to create raving fan customers. The only way you do that is to create Gung Ho people. Finally, you need to teach people that they have the autonomy to care for and feed their own monkeys—they don't have to pass them up the hierarchy.

Anyone who reads these five books is bound to become a better manager with happier people and more satisfied customers. I hope you enjoy these stories and that you, your people, your customers, and your organization benefit from their simple but powerful truths.

KEN BLANCHARD, SAN DIEGO, CALIFORNIA

PROLOGUE

by Peggy Sinclair

Now a promise made is a debt unpaid...

ROBERT W. SERVICE

"The Cremation of Sam McGee"

Tuesday I made my promise to Andy Longclaw.

I promised to tell you how we saved our business from closure. How we then made record profits, with record productivity. How you too can motivate and turn on the power of your whole workforce. But first, I want to tell you why I made this promise, and how this book came to be written. It all began at Walton Memorial Hospital, June 7, 1994.

Andy was in the hospital. We both knew it would be our last visit, but I couldn't bring myself to admit he was going, or to tell him the things I needed to say. Instead I chatted brightly about the spring day, baseball, and business.

In mid-sentence I stopped. I'd just run out of small talk. There was, for me, a short and awkward silence. Then I heard my thoughts break through.

"I love you, Andy," I choked out.

His large weathered hand moved slowly across the sheet and covered mine with a grip that was still surprisingly strong.

"I know," he said. Then added, "I love you too. Always have."

Whether it was the emotion of the moment, or my visit, that had worn him out, I don't know. But he closed his eyes. His head rested easily on the pillow. I knew he wasn't asleep. His hand still held mine in a reassuring grip. He may simply have been honoring the moment with silence. I had learned over the years that a long silence from Andy was his way of telling me that what I'd said was important. It deserved its own space before being banished by a reply.

We sat together, our hands touching, for several minutes. Andy once told me his mother had taught him not to wait for silence before speaking, but rather to wait for the silence to end. Finally Andy spoke, his voice clear but weak. "I will be leaving today to join my ancestors." As always, he tackled the issue head-on.

I didn't reply, but no reply was necessary as he continued, "You have blessed me with pride and riches."

"Oh no, Andy. No," I protested. "It is you who have blessed me and everyone in the company."

"We have done much together," Andy said with wisdom and finality.

Then he added, "There is still much to be done. Too many toil alone. They are unhappy. Their spirits die at the office door."

I gave Andy's hand a gentle squeeze. *Their spirits die at the office door.* How true. All across America, spirits died at the office door.

"You must tell the story so our children can tell their children." Andy paused, and took several deep breaths before continuing.

"The Gung Ho story. *The Spirit of the Squirrel, the Way of the Beaver, the Gift of the Goose.*"

"I will, Andy. I will. I promise."

"Thank you," he replied. "You have lifted my last burden."

Then he added, "The owl calls my name and waits to lead me on. I will go while there is still light." He looked over at me and smiled with a look of tranquillity I'll never forget.

"Gung Ho, friend."

"Gung Ho, friend," I replied.

Gung Ho had been our special greeting and our good-bye for many years. This was to be our last.

He closed his eyes. This time he slept. His breathing became slow and shallow. His grip relaxed.

I knew that no matter what the doctors might say or do, before sunset Andy's life on this plane would be over. He had decided to go, and he would.

I don't know how long I sat with him or when he died. His spirit answered the owl's call so gently, the transition passed without notice. At some point I realized he was gone.

I slipped my hand out from under his, and with tears pouring from my eyes I stood up, bent over, and kissed him silently good-bye.

The smile was still on his face.

I don't remember leaving the room, or calling the nurse. I do remember walking away from the hospital, wondering how I would keep my promise. How would I tell our story? *The Spirit of the Squirrel, the Way of the Beaver, the Gift of the Goose.* The three revelations that led to our success.

Some event was ending at the auditorium next to the hospital. As I waited for the traffic light to change, I sensed the presence of two men who walked up behind me. Lost in my own thoughts I didn't hear their conversation, but suddenly, something one said came through loud and clear: "The Buddhists say, when the student is ready, the teacher will appear."

Perhaps, I thought, as the light changed and I started across the street, the answer to my promise would appear.

I didn't want to go home and I wasn't prepared to return to the office. On the corner was a Denny's Restaurant. Not knowing what else to do I entered and ordered coffee. Whenever I thought of Andy I began to cry again and so I tried to concentrate on the promise I had made and how I might tell the story. The Gung Ho story.

Andy and the owl must have paused long enough on their journey to set the wheels of coincidence in motion.

INTRODUCTION

by

Ken Blanchard

and

Sheldon Bowles

The hand of fate,
Happy coincidence,
Two hours early, ten late
That's the difference!

MANLY GRANT
Collected Verse, Volume II

Our seminar in Walton began at noon Tuesday and would finish on Wednesday morning. We'd ended our first session and decided to walk across the street to Denny's for an early dinner.

Since the two of us co-authored *Raving Fans!: A Revolutionary Approach to Customer Service*, we had found there was also a real need for a companion book: a book on how to turn employees into raving fans of the organization they worked for. A lot of organizations were trying to create Raving Fan Service® with tired, uninspired, and even resentful employees. It was a formula destined to fail. Worse, these employees hated to go to work. What a waste of a day—or at least eight hours of one.

Our literary agent, Margret McBride, and our editor, Larry Hughes, were keen on the project, but not about our proposed title: *Raving Employees.*

"Foaming at the mouth!" was Margret's comment.

"A workers' rights riot," grumped Larry.

The title wasn't our big problem, however. A piece of the puzzle was missing. Like physicists we knew lots of answers but didn't have a Grand Unified Theory.

We had been excited at the prospect of coming to Walton, home of Walton Works #2, perhaps the most famous business turnaround story in America. Unfortunately our appointment to interview the factory's General Manager, Peggy Sinclair, had been canceled. A close friend and co-worker of hers was very ill. She had sent her regrets and we were disappointed.

Peggy Sinclair was a legend. When she had taken over Walton Works #2 the plant was the worst of the thirty-two the company owned. Now it ran so well the White House had recognized it as one of the nation's finest workplaces.

The efficiency, the profitability, the innovations and creativity, the Raving Fans Service® delivered to customers, all traced back to one thing—a workforce ready, willing, able, and eager to take on fresh challenges and to work together for the common good. In short, what we thought of as Raving Employees.

As we walked to Denny's we discussed our problem. If we were ever to find our missing key, our Grand Unified Theory of Everything, Peggy Sinclair might be our best hope and now we were going to miss her. Who knew when we'd get back to Walton? Our calendars were booked months in advance.

"The Buddhists say, when the student is ready, the teacher will appear," one of us observed philosophically as the light changed and we crossed to Denny's. We didn't pay any attention to the woman who entered the restaurant ahead of us. It wasn't until our meal was served that we noticed her. She was sitting alone across the restaurant. Even tear-streaked, Peggy Sinclair's face was easily recognizable from the photo in the publicity package the White House had sent us on the Walton Works #2 award.

At that very same moment she looked up and recognized us as well. To our surprise she stood up and walked over to our table. We struggled to our feet with the self-conscious awkwardness that always accompanies intruding on a stranger's privacy in a time of personal stress.

"I'm Peggy Sinclair," she said bravely. "I recognize the two of you. I'm sorry I couldn't keep our appointment today. It's been... Well, it's been a bad day for me."

Not knowing what to do or say we fell back on the traditional courtesy of asking her to join us, fully expecting her to thank us and depart. She again surprised us. After a slight hesitation, she accepted.

The following story is an account of what we learned sitting at that table for the next three hours and in many other meetings in the months that followed. We would often meet at an airport hotel as our paths crossed and Peggy could join us.

When the student is ready, the teacher will appear.

Gung Ho!

THE GUNG HO STORY

The woods are lovely, dark and deep.
But I have promises to keep,
And miles to go before I sleep,
And miles to go before I sleep.

ROBERT FROST

"Stopping by Woods on a Snowy Evening"

I'd been set up.

Me, Peggy Sinclair, head-office rising star!

I should have realized it when Old Man Morris told me I'd been named General Manager of Walton Works #2.

The excitement of getting my own plant blinded me to what must have been obvious to everyone else. I'd never been in operations before. Always in a staff position. I knew the theory all right but I'd never done it. I wasn't trained or ready to run a plant. Even one doing well. And this one wasn't.

I thought I'd been forgiven for the staff study I'd authored which concluded that Old Man Morris's new strategic plan had a fatal flaw. He wasn't happy. But he acknowledged the problem and this saved the company $1 million. I thought Walton Works #2 was my reward. It was—just not the way I had it figured.

Tuesday, September 4, 8:00 A.M., I arrived at the Walton Works #2 plant full of energy and enthusiasm. By quitting time it was clear that I'd been had. Everyone knew the plant was the worst in the system. But I had never imagined anything this bad. The plant survived only because of the antiquated way our head office cost-accounted, and that was changing. This plant was in major trouble.

Six months, a year at the most, and it would be closing. Gone! And I'd be going with it. The perfect scapegoat for Walton Works #2.

It didn't take a genius to see why productivity was so low. The company treated the raw material piled in the yard better than it treated the workers.

As I met with my management team, I found only one bright spot: the 150-person finishing department. In spite of the problems with Walton Works #2, no other department in our whole thirty-two-plant system was so efficient! That meant about 10 percent of this plant's workforce were gems. The rest appeared to be lumps of coal managed by Neanderthals intent on self-destruction.

Then, when I met with the Division Manager to whom the manager of the finishing department reported, I was told all wasn't well, even there.

"You'll want to get rid of the operations manager there fast," the Division Manager advised.

"Really? Why?" I questioned. I also wondered why this was my responsibility and not his, but right then I was mainly interested in why this operations manager should be fired.

"Andy Longclaw is bad news. Indian guy, you know. Now, I've nothing against Indians and this one's a bright brave. No doubt about that. Got an MBA even. But he's a troublemaker. Real thorn in the side. That department will be even better once he's gone. Indians!" he added with evident distaste. His next comment was far worse.

I didn't know if Andy Longclaw was a troublemaker or not. But I did know this Division Manager wasn't going to last while I was around. I might be fired myself in six months, but I didn't have to spend it in the presence of narrow-minded fools like him.

At day's end, come 4:30, the office emptied out so quickly you'd have sworn the fire alarm had gone off. I hung around another half hour, then left myself.

There was still plenty of daylight left, so I decided to take a long walk. I started down Main Street. I didn't have a destination. I was just wandering and thinking. I noted the town had two supermarkets, two drugstores, and a statue in front of the town library. Reading the inscription I discovered that unlike the statues in most towns, it didn't honor a famous warrior or long-dead politician, but instead an artist. Apparently Walton had been home to Andrew Payton, a Native American wood-carver, who had won a number of international awards for his beautiful wildlife carvings.

I continued to Seventh and crossed the bridge. A green field led to the river edge and a lone bench sat looking across the river to where the factory stood grim and lifeless. A good metaphor, I decided, for what was happening inside.

I started down toward the bench, thinking I didn't have any idea of how to turn the factory around. I knew I was a fast learner. It was the only positive I could think of. Trouble was, I didn't even know where to begin.

As I neared the bench, a tall, dark-haired man, ambling along from the other direction, flopped down, hands thrust deep in his pockets. He'd taken the far end of the bench. Normally I'd have been wary of sitting next to a stranger, but I felt the safety of a small town.

"Mind if I sit down?"

"Sure thing. But I'm afraid I'm not very good company today."

"Troubles?" I asked, more from politeness than caring.

"Expect I'm going to be fired," the man answered with that charming frankness that can exist between total strangers.

"How come?" I ventured, glad for the distraction from my own troubles.

"I work at the plant over there. At least today I worked there. Have for the past fifteen years. Tomorrow though, who knows?"

"You haven't said why."

"Boss says I'm going. Doesn't have the guts to let me go himself. Worried about the backlash, I guess."

"Backlash?"

"Yeah. But I don't really think there'd be much backlash. The guys in my department know that the factory is on its last legs. We give it six months to a year. Not much sense in fussing about me going. We've got a bit of a reputation as a feisty bunch though, so he's scared."

I looked at my benchmate with new interest. I guessed from his features he was a Native American,[*]

---

[*]The aboriginal peoples of North America refer to themselves in many unique ways. In *Gung Ho!* the authors and Peggy use the term Native American. But when Andy speaks, or happenings from fifteen to twenty years ago are quoted, the term Indian is used. Both are used with honor and respect. We trust they will be so received by readers.

and I suspected I knew who this was. It was obvious from his next comment that he had no idea who I was.

"Some new lady's taking over," he continued. "A real Wicked Witch of the West, we hear. Boss says she's going to fire me and I expect she will. Fifteen years. I guess I shouldn't care. The place isn't going to last long anyway. Don't know what will happen to the town when it's gone. Six months. Tomorrow. Shouldn't make a difference, but it does. I'd sort of like to leave along with my guys on the last day. We've got a goal."

"A goal?"

"Sure do," he replied with a broad grin. "We're working up to it. Our last day is going to be a record day for efficiency and productivity. When we go out that gate for the last time, we're going with our heads held high. Kinda like to be there."

I knew now without a doubt who this stranger was. And I loved his idea of ending with your head held high. The last day being the most efficient, most productive day. In an instant I decided I might be going down myself, but I was going down fighting!

"You don't look too happy yourself," he said.

"I expect I'm going to be fired."

"You're kidding."

"I don't kid about being fired. My boss wants to get rid of me and I expect he's going to get his way."

"You too? Where do you work?"

"That plant over there."

"Really? I don't remember seeing you. I know we've got fifteen hundred people, but I thought I knew most of the faces. What do you do?"

"Do?" I replied and gave him my best impish grin. "Do? Why I'm the Wicked Witch of the West and I'll bet you're Andy Longclaw. I've heard about you. Nothing good, I might add."

Andy let out a groan that began rumbling at his toes and reverberated out his head.

"That does it. I'm one dead Indian. I'm outta here!"

"Not by *my* hand," I said. "The only termination I'm considering for your department is to get rid of one very bigoted Division Manager who wants to fire someone who is probably the best person I've got in the plant—Andy Longclaw."

Andy looked at me astonished.

"You putting me on?"

"I may be the Wicked Witch of the West but I'm no fool."

"You'll keep me?"

"Of course. You run the best department I've got."

"You're kidding about your being fired though, aren't you?"

"Wish I was," and I told him the story. Sounds odd, I know. But there I was, telling a total stranger everything. Somehow I knew that I could trust him, that he was someone special. Then I asked the question that would save Walton Works #2.

"Tell me. That finishing department of yours seems to run like a clock in the midst of disaster. How come?"

"Gung Ho. We're all Gung Ho."

"Gung Ho? You mean excited? Turned on?"

"Exactly. We're Gung Ho."

"Working in that plant? For your Division Manager?"

"He doesn't make it any easier. But we're all Gung Ho."

"And you're responsible for that?"

"Not me. My grandfather."

"He works in the plant?"

"No way. He never even saw the inside of the plant. He's been dead for ten years. But I became head of the finishing department two years before he died, and he taught me Gung Ho. I teach it to the guys—excuse me, the women too, we've got lots of women in my department—and so we're all Gung Ho."

"Could we teach it to the rest of the plant?"

"Absolutely. Just one problem."

"Which is?"

"Took me five years to get the finishing department Gung Ho. I figure you've got six months to a year."

"You're right about that," I sadly agreed.

"Too bad," Andy said. "Doing the whole plant would be fun."

"If you've done it once, couldn't you teach me how to do it faster the second time?"

Andy paused so long I thought he was ignoring me. Then he said, "Three years. Minimum three years."

"But at best we've got one year, Andy," I said, almost pleading.

"Three years to full Gung Ho. But some change in one year."

"Enough to save the plant?"

"Who knows?"

"Want to try?"

"Beats being fired, I guess."

"Sure does. Besides, being fired would look bad on your résumé next to that MBA I hear you have."

"Right. Good point. Gung Ho."

"Gung Ho, Andy Longclaw. I'm Peggy Sinclair," and I stuck out my hand. He took it and shaking it said, "Gung Ho, friend."

From that time on, whenever we met or parted, the salutation was always the same: "Gung Ho, friend."

"One thing puzzles me," I said, releasing Andy's hand.

"Just one?" he said with a warm laugh.

"Just one right now. Tell me, if you've got an MBA and the ability to do what you've done in the finishing department, why have you stayed here? Seems to me you could work anywhere and in lots better jobs."

When Andy gave me the answer I was sorry I'd asked. Inadvertently I'd opened an old wound. His reason was unique and deeply personal, but he didn't hesitate to tell me.

Andy said his wife and son were buried in Walton. His wife had been taking their son home after school when they were hit by a drunken driver in the middle of the afternoon. "We'd planned to move along after I had a few years of hands-on management experience. But when they stayed, I did too."

"I'm sorry."

"Me too. It was a long time ago, but most nights it still hurts."

I didn't know what to say next and so I sat quietly and let time fill the gap between us.

Eventually I asked, "Well, if we're going to Gung Ho that place"—my arm waved toward the factory across the river—"how do we start?"

"Spirit of the Squirrel," he replied. "It all begins with the Spirit of the Squirrel. Later comes Way of the Beaver and Gift of the Goose. I'm off shift at three-thirty tomorrow. Meet me at the main gate. Wear slacks. We'll be going out into the country."

He rose to his feet, looked me in the eye, and said, "Gung Ho, friend."

"Gung Ho, friend," I replied.

He turned and walked off the way he had come, never once looking back. He had a bounce in his step that wasn't there earlier.

It was a strange start to a productive friendship that led us eventually to the Rose Garden at the White House and an award for our Gung Ho efforts.

Years later someone once suggested that our friendship was cemented because we were both underdogs in society. I a woman. Andy an Indian. That wasn't it at all. *I* might have been an underdog. In those days I was still trying to decide if I wanted to be known as Miss or Ms. Not Andy. He knew who he was and what he wanted to be called. Andy wore Indian as a badge of honor. There was nothing underdog about Andy.

He once told me his grandfather liked to say, "If you're not lead dog the scenery never changes." Andy was lead dog all the way.

The next morning I toured most of the factory before the midnight shift left. "Never had no General Manager on the midnight shift before," said the foreman when I discovered him playing cards in the shop-floor office and asked for a tour. At 8:00 A.M. I had the day foreman repeat the tour.

Because I'd worked the floor when I was putting myself through college, I knew the process inside out.

The foremen, I could tell, were good, knowledgeable people. They just didn't much care.

If the foremen were surprised to find me on the shop floor, my Division Managers were apoplectic. About midway through the second tour they arrived en masse. Like a pack of sheepdogs they started yapping at my heels, determined to herd me back to the office area.

"We could brief you in the Boardroom. . . ."

"I could better explain back at the office where we have everything on file. . . ."

"You really need to see the graph on my wall. . . ."

When they understood I wasn't going back, the tour continued. However, all meaningful information ended.

They were genuinely relieved when I suggested they all go back to the office. The only department left was the finishing department. I wanted to give that Division Manager a chance to redeem himself, so I suggested he come along.

With my least favorite Division Manager at my side I entered the finishing department. This was, he said, the prototype shop of tomorrow. Some real problems, of course, with that Andy Longclaw fellow he'd told me about.

"Won't follow orders. These people in here could be working a lot harder. I've told him to cut three minutes off each coffee break but he hasn't done it. Slackers too. Won't get rid of them."

Up on the walls I saw Gung Ho signs, and most machines had Gung Ho stickers on them.

"What is this Gung Ho?" I asked my guide casually.

He peered at the signs with some surprise, as if he had never seen them before and I doubt he had. "Don't know," he admitted. "Probably some subversive Indian slogan," he concluded.

"Andy Longclaw?"

"That's the guy. Probably trying to subvert a revolution."

"*Subvert* a revolution?"

"I wouldn't be a bit surprised."

Andy was nowhere to be seen. I learned later he had been warned of our arrival—"Grassroots tomtom," he explained—and had deliberately slipped away.

This really was a department like no other in the plant. It was spotlessly clean, and the workers (it wasn't until later I learned to call them team members) were in bright, clean uniforms and work in progress was organized in a neat, orderly fashion. In addition to the Gung Ho signs, there were all kinds of charts, graphs, and record boards reporting progress by all sorts of different measures.

Most of all I noticed the atmosphere. People were happy. The gloom in the rest of the factory was real and evident. The optimism here was every bit as real.

The Division Manager sealed his fate when he wondered why an Indian had been hired in the first place when there were "lots of honest white men available."

Not the brightest thing to say to anyone, much less to me, a woman. But it never occurred to him. I'd have been angry if I hadn't felt sorry for him. Narrow minds lived narrow lives, I'd learned.

First order of business when I returned to my office wasn't a pleasant one. With a generous severance package I parted company with one of the eighteen Division Managers I'd inherited. I believe anyone can grow and change, but I didn't have enough time to work with this person. Sometimes the only way to change a manager is to change a manager.

When I met with the remaining seventeen I told them two things:

"First, if you're going to quit, then leave. The quit-but-stay option is over." Looks of alarm and shock swept around the room as they realized I was dead serious.

They found my second bit of news equally disquieting. I'd be leaving early that afternoon and would be out for the balance of the day chasing squirrel spirits.

The Division Managers filed out of my office in silence. Their morning shock escalated that afternoon when I noticed seventeen startled faces at office windows as I rode out the plant's main gate perched precariously on the back of Andy Longclaw's Harley-Davidson.

I let out a whoop of delight as Andy yelled, "Hang on. We're off!"

If you had told me the previous week that I'd be clinging to the back of a Native American, flying down the highway on his motorcycle and loving every minute of it, I'd have laughed and said, totally impossible. A suggestion that I'd also be placing my future in the hands of his grandfather's management theories, apparently rooted in squirrels, beavers, and geese, would have been so ridiculous as to be beyond totally impossible. Yet here I was doing exactly that and somehow I knew I was doing the right thing. Gung Ho was my only chance to save myself and the plant.

We soon left the highway and headed into the countryside. I judged we were about fifteen miles from town when Andy turned into a dirt driveway and stopped in a clearing some five hundred feet into the woods off the country road.

"We're here," said Andy as he shut down the Harley.

We were in the midst of a magnificent spruce forest. Close by stood a small log cabin with a wide front porch and fieldstone chimney.

The silence was beautiful. I began to walk slowly toward the cabin, letting my senses take in what was truly a magical place. "It's wonderful," I said turning to Andy. I stopped dead. There, just behind him, no more than one hundred feet, a doe and fawn picked their way across the clearing and into the bush on the other side.

I pointed urgently. Andy turned and looked at the deer.

"That's Mabel and Fred," he said.

"Mabel and Fred!"

"Well, that's what I call them," he said defensively. "I've a salt lick by that tree. They come by several times a day."

Andy led me up onto the porch, got us both a cold beer, and sat me down in a large old-fashioned rocking chair. He flopped down in the hammock.

"Time to discover the Spirit of the Squirrel," Andy announced. I looked at him expectantly.

"You watch the squirrels. I'm going to have a nap."

"I thought you were going to teach me about the Spirit of the Squirrel."

"Not exactly. You're going to learn. I'm going to have a nap. Lots of squirrels around. Tell me what you've learned when I wake up."

With that, Andy closed his eyes and was soon snoring gently. I was left to watch the squirrels! This man was either the most self-assured person I'd ever met or absolutely crazy. I was the new boss. I'd met him just the day before. And here he was asleep!

I wondered briefly if I was being had. But no. I remembered the Gung Ho feeling in the finishing department. He said it began with Spirit of the Squirrel. If he said to watch squirrels, then I'd watch squirrels. He might be crazy but I'd already made my choice and cast my future with his.

Andy was right about the squirrels. They were all over the place. Just off the porch was a flat plywood feeder, sitting on a stump. Squirrels came scurrying out of the woods, across the lawn, and up onto the feeder. They would then fill their cheeks with sunflower seeds and head back to the forest.

I began timing the squirrels I recognized and discovered on average they were working a three-minute, fifty-second round trip. Roughly sixteen trips an hour. No wonder Andy supplied the feeder automatically by chute from an overhead bin.

"Well," came Andy's voice from the hammock at the end of an hour, "what have you learned?"

"I'm not sure I've learned the Spirit of the Squirrel, but if people at Walton Works #2 worked anything like these squirrels, that factory would be booming."

"I agree," said Andy as he slowly rocked the hammock. I waited for Andy to continue but he remained silent.

"So, how do we do that?" I finally asked.

"*Spirit of the Squirrel, Way of the Beaver, Gift of the Goose.* Gung Ho."

"We've been here before," I said with a laugh. "Let's just stick with these squirrels for now."

"Suits me. The question is: Why do those squirrels work so hard? Find the answer to that and you've discovered the Spirit of the Squirrel."

"They work hard because they are motivated," I ventured.

"Good. Excellent. And why are they motivated?"

"They have a goal. They are working toward the goal of putting away food," I said.

"And why does that goal motivate them?" asked Andy.

We both rocked while I thought.

"They're motivated because if they don't store up food they won't survive the winter. They'll die."

"Now you're beginning to understand the Spirit of the Squirrel."

"The point you're making then is: There's more to the squirrel's work than just moving seed. They are motivated because the work is important."

"Their work goes beyond important. It's *worthwhile*," said Andy, putting heavy emphasis on the word "worthwhile," as he climbed out of the hammock and ambled into the cabin.

He returned, saying he had a gift for me. He handed me a carving of a squirrel, standing erect, mouth open, chattering. I could hear the scolding. Every hair of the squirrel's coat seemed to be detailed and I could see the muscles ripple in its powerful hind legs.

"Andy. It's magnificent. Where did you ever get it?"

"Grandfather carved it when he taught me Gung Ho. Turn it over."

I did so and discovered burned into the wooden base the carver's name, Andrew Payton, the date, July 1967, and the following:

—

The Spirit of the Squirrel:

Worthwhile work

—

There it was. The first secret that had turned the finishing department into a Gung Ho team and would save Walton Works #2. At the time I didn't realize just how powerful it would be.

"Your grandfather was Andrew Payton? I saw his statue."

"Ironic, isn't it? He carved in wood and they did him in bronze."

"It's beautiful," I said, examining the carving closely. "It's a wonderful gift, Andy, but I can't accept this. Your grandfather carved it for you."

Andy smiled. "True. But Gung Ho was his gift to Walton Works #2. I have a number of his carvings. Grandfather would have wanted you to have it."

"Thank you," I replied and again looked at the message his grandfather had burned into the base: THE SPIRIT OF THE SQUIRREL: WORTHWHILE WORK.

"Worthwhile," I said aloud as I turned the idea over in my mind.

"Squirrels work hard because their work is worthwhile. It works for people too," said Andy as he again settled into his hammock. "Worthwhile goes beyond important but it starts with important."

"You've said twice that worthwhile goes beyond important. How can something be more important than important?"

"Worthwhile doesn't mean more important than important," Andy replied with a chuckle. "Worthwhile just covers more territory than important. There are three lessons to learn: First, the work has to be understood as important. Second, it has to lead to a well-understood and shared goal. Third, values have to guide all plans, decisions, and actions. Put all three together and you've got worthwhile work. In short, Spirit of the Squirrel.

"But, as I said, it starts with important. If you want people to be Gung Ho, to work with the Spirit of the Squirrel, they must first of all understand why they are needed. Why their work makes the world a better place.

"Grandfather said:

—

The Spirit of the Squirrel Fulfills God's Plan for the Forest.

—

"People have to understand how what they do contributes to the well-being of humankind—makes a difference in their own patch of forest."

The impact of Andy's words made me tingle with excitement. We had lots of incentive programs in our company. Carrots pulled you forward. Sticks chased you from behind. But no incentive matched this. Imagine doing work so important it changed the course of the world. Work that fulfilled God's plan.

My euphoria was short-lived. I remembered the product we made. Important? Well, to some folks it was, but it hardly seemed part of God's plan.

Andy was watching me. He knew my objection before I voiced it.

"It's the understanding. It's not the work itself. Most any job you can name is important and makes the world a better place to live. People really are needed. It's just that they don't understand how they fit in.

"Grandfather said that once people understand, their work becomes right work, and people need right work to be Gung Ho," he said.

"I like the idea, Andy, but I have trouble when you say most any job is important and makes the world a better place."

"Of course you do," agreed Andy. "We've all been trained to see work as units. Units started, units polished, units finished, units sold, or units whatever."

"That's how we measure things," I acknowledged.

"We do. And so we think that units dealt with is the reason we work. It takes a different mind-set to go beyond that. You have to learn to see how what you've done has helped others."

"How can most jobs be so important that they change the world? Nurses in hospitals, relief workers, the scientists working for drug companies I can see. But. . .?" I let the question hang.

"Like I said, it's a different mind-set. It's learning to see what you do, what you're accomplishing, in people terms. Tell me: What's the most meaningless job you've ever had or can think of?"

"That's easy. I washed dishes in the cafeteria at college. I assure you it wasn't meaningful work."

Dishwashing, I knew, was as meaningless as work could ever be. I remembered trays of dirty dishes coming in on the conveyor belt. I scraped, I put them in the washer. I piled the clean ones. I was confident the work was meaningless, but the smile on Andy's face also made me slightly uneasy.

"Dishwashing in a college cafeteria—it just doesn't get more important than that. My God, think of the impact those students were going to have on the world. Business leaders, doctors, social scientists, world leaders, researchers. One load of unclean, bacteria-infected dishes could have wiped out a whole class. Look at it in terms of human impact. Not units dealt with. If you don't believe dishwashing contributes to the well-being of humankind, I can take you to a couple of spots in the world where dishes don't always get properly washed. One meal will quickly change your mind.

"Students arrived tired, hungry, and likely lonely. You were an important part of the chain that provided joy and nourishment in their lives. What a wonderful gift to give another human being."

Then Andy looked me directly in the eye and said, "Our whole economy depends on mobility. Being able to participate beyond the range of our picnic baskets. Sanitary eating conditions, clean dishes, eating safely away from home—that's at the very foundation of our civilization."

"I guess it all depends on how you look at it," I replied somewhat defensively.

"It all depends on looking at it clearly," said Andy firmly.

"And this gets people Gung Ho," I said, half as a question, half as a statement of fact.

"It's the beginning. Most any job has social value—and that's a phrase Grandfather used too—be it digging ditches, answering telephones, designing golf courses, or manufacturing wire baskets. Once people begin to see their work clearly, big things begin to happen. Bashing a chunk of metal and grinding it into conformity with an engineering drawing is one thing. Making a part for a brake on a child's bicycle is entirely different."

After a pause Andy said, "Mess up the first and you're off spec. Mess up the second and you might break a child's leg or worse."

"The first is units dealt with, the second is right work, isn't it, Andy?"

He smiled in agreement. "What we're really talking about is one of the most powerful human emotions. It ranks right up there with love and hate. It's called self-esteem. One of the fastest and surest ways to feel good about yourself is to understand how your work fits into the big picture. When you feel good about yourself, well, that's the beginning of Gung Ho."

The still peace of a late summer afternoon settled over the porch as Andy began talking about how our factory served both our customers and the community. He spoke quietly but with such insight, I soon began to see our company in a new way. I understood how our work touched people and how important it was. For the first time I saw our product as something more than units produced.

When I'd entered Andy's clearing I'd known it was a magical place. But here was magic of a whole different order.

"The Spirit of the Squirrel is just what we need, Andy. Gung Ho, here we come."

"Whoa! Hold your horses," said Andy with a smile. "We're not finished. Remember, worthwhile means more than important."

"Okay. What's next?"

"All in good time. Right now it's time to wake up head office. You wait here." Andy heaved himself to his feet and went into his cabin. He emerged with a couple of slices of bread and a plastic bag of table scraps. "Garbage. Old garbage. That's what head office likes best. You watch."

About fifty feet off the porch he put his offering on the ground. Nearby a steel triangle hung from a tree and Andy gave this gong a few sharp raps with an iron bar. He scurried back up on the porch considerably faster than he'd gone down.

"Watch the feeding shed," said Andy. "The President and all the Vice Presidents will be right out."

In stately procession from under the shed emerged a black animal with two white stripes down its back. Three small ones followed.

"Skunks and more skunks!" I hooted with laughter.

"Quiet," pleaded Andy. "Don't laugh at head office. They'll kick up a hell of a stink if you annoy them."

The skunks soon finished their meal. Mother skunk—at least I assumed it was mother, I wasn't about to check—turned and headed back to the shed. The others quickly fell in behind.

"They'll be back out later. They like night the best," said Andy just as a squirrel mounted the feeder and, with arched back and tail stuck straight into the air, delivered a loud, long tongue-lashing.

"You might call the skunks head office, but the squirrel sounds like Old Man Morris to me."

"He's just jealous because I've stopped telling you about Spirit of the Squirrel and given some attention to the skunks," said Andy in all seriousness. Then, with shrill volume and intensity to match the lecture from the squirrel, Andy delivered a rebuttal that sounded so much like a squirrel, the squirrel fell silent.

"There. That ought to hold the cheeky rascal for a while. I promised him I'd tell you about goals and values."

Andy delivered this information with all the matter-of-fact calmness you or I would have in answering a telephone, turning to a co-worker, and saying, "It's for you."

Andy may have been putting me on, but he certainly mimicked the squirrel perfectly. And the squirrel must have got the message, since he promptly shut up and began to gather seeds.

True to his promise to the squirrel, Andy continued my lesson.

"You can't have worthwhile work unless everyone is working toward a well-understood and shared goal. But that's not enough. It matters how you reach the goal. You must be guided by values. You have to be proud of both the goal and how you get there."

I was still watching the squirrel and I swear the animal was listening to be sure that Andy was keeping his promise. Andy took my silence as a signal to go on.

"Goal setting is a big problem in most organizations. The managers think because they print a goal in the annual report or announce it at some meeting, the goal is shared. They may have shared it, but if the team doesn't commit, it isn't a shared goal."

"You can lead a horse to water but you can't make him drink," I observed.

"That's it. If the horse doesn't drink, it just isn't shared water. It's the buy-in that makes the difference. It's the commitment to making the goal a reality that has to be shared. Those squirrels are all committed to the same goal. In Gung Ho organizations it's the same with people."

"I understand."

"Glad you do. Most people don't," said Andy. "When I first started at Walton Works #2 we had lots of goals and objectives. One General Manager even had a pep rally, complete with T-shirts and a company song.

"The only problem was, no one cared about the goals. We were singing because it was a good party on a hot afternoon and the beer was cold. Then management wondered why nothing changed. Sometimes I think stupidity is the main talent required to get ahead in our company," Andy snorted.

The surprise must have shown on my face.

"Sorry about that," he said sheepishly. "I didn't mean you. My wife used to say I've been grumpy since I was a boy and discovered the cowboys always beat the Indians in the Saturday afternoon movie."

I was to learn that Andy, while intensely proud of his Indian heritage, was comfortable enough with who he was and had sufficient self-esteem to poke fun at himself as well.

"I guess people get mixed up between shared support and shared awareness," I said.

"They sure do," said Andy. "Good lesson to be learned from those skunks. Their goal is to control the whole yard. I'm aware of it, but I don't share it. Not by a long shot."

"I'll get working on goals," I promised.

"Do that. But don't forget that sometimes the best way to lead is to find out where people are going anyway and then get out front. It's my job to set goals for the finishing department, but the fact is, of ten goals only two or three are critical. I can let the team set the rest on their own."

Although we didn't discuss it that day, as we worked to Gung Ho the plant, Andy taught me that I needed to have two types of goals:

First, *result goals.* Statements that set out where we wanted to be—whether it was units worked on, finished, or shipped, or accounts collected, or whatever.

Second, *value goals.* Statements that set out the impact we wanted to have on the lives of our team members, our customers, our suppliers, and our community.

I also later learned that goals are marker posts you drive into the future landscape between where you are and where you want to be. They focus attention productively.

"So, worthwhile work means understanding how the work makes the world a better place, and it's also work that helps achieve a well-understood and shared goal," I said. "And the third item on your list was values?" I questioned Andy.

"Importance and goals get people going. It's values that sustain the effort. There is nothing worthwhile about work that leads to a goal arrived at by cheating. I can't tell you all the values squirrels have, but I do know they have them. For example, they value the lives of one another. If a hawk or fox comes around, they don't save just themselves. They chatter a warning to the others. To be Gung Ho you have to have values."

"So, where do these values come from? From the team or from management?" I asked.

"Both. But values are more management's unique responsibility than goal setting is. With goals, you will have a couple of critical ones. With values, every one is critical.

"You can compromise and negotiate on goals. Sometimes the fastest route to where you want to get isn't a straight line. But with values there are only straight lines. Leaders have to insist that everyone follow the straight line."

Andy paused and let this sink in before he continued. "In a Gung Ho organization values are the real boss. Values are to guide your behavior, not for you to guide others. You're a leader, not the police. At the same time, though, you have to ensure the organization is internally aligned—everyone singing from the same hymn book. You can't impose agreement to values any more than you can to goals, but you can, and must, impose conformity. If people don't respect your values, then they work elsewhere. You wouldn't keep someone who didn't work for your result goals. Don't keep people who won't honor your values either."

"I've already done that today," I pointed out. I'd told Andy earlier that his Division Manager and I had parted company.

"Yes, you have, haven't you?" said Andy. "I'm sure you'll stick to your values in the future too. Once you proclaim a value, you can't toss it aside just because it might be inconvenient."

"I can't see that being a problem," I said.

"Usually it isn't. But sometimes a value has unforeseen consequences. For example, one of our values in the finishing department is to respect the dignity of work. Sounds like a great idea and it is. But we discovered, as we improved our productivity, some folks' performance was left behind. It wasn't because they didn't try or didn't care. The rest of us had just gone beyond these people's capacity to fully participate. Problem was: What do we do with them?"

"I see the problem. Tough call."

"Not really, when you think it through. If we truly value the dignity of work, we have to respect everyone's right to work. So we decided that as long as a person was working to their level of ability and not goofing off, we wouldn't deny them the dignity of work. We may put them in a different position where they can continue to contribute, but we keep them. They have the dignity of work. It's one of our core values."

"That explains why you've got some low-performing people. Your late Division Manager claimed you could raise productivity two points by clearing out the deadwood."

"He was wrong on two counts," laughed Andy. "First, they likely cost us closer to three points. Second, if we cleared them out, we'd soon be rid of all our values and that would be the end of Gung Ho, so productivity would be down seventeen points. We'd be right in there with the rest of the plant!"

"Good point," I acknowledged.

"That's the thing about a value. It has to hold up in tough times. Otherwise it's not a value. It's a feel-good slogan of the day. It's ethics of convenience."

"So, values are set by leaders. Perhaps with some consultation. Then, as you said, values are the boss."

"They have to be," said Andy. "If your values are not the boss, Gung Ho will never take hold."

Andy's next lesson was an important one. "Let's back up a moment. You said, 'Values are set by leaders.' Values aren't set the way goals are. The minute, the second, you proclaim a goal it's real. It's set. Values don't work that way. You can proclaim a value all you want, and you need to do that, but values become real only when you demonstrate them in the way you act and the way you insist others behave. Goals are for the future. Values are now. Goals are set. Values are lived. Goals change. Values are rocks you can count on.

"Grandfather said, 'Rocks don't move in a swirling river. Pebbles roll. Even if you call them rocks.'"

I made a comment about how wise his grandfather was. Andy laughed and said, "Wisest person I've ever known. But like most wise people, he learned from others. I think he picked up on rocks and pebbles from one of his favorite poets, Manly Grant. I'll show you."

Andy brought me a book from the cabin and, opening it at one of several markers, showed me a poem:

Hold or Roll

Rocks hold firm while water's might
Sends pebbles rolling left and right.
Call pebbles rock? Set firm their goal?
First flash flood, still pebbles roll.
Not name, nor goal divide the two.
It's how they act. It's what they do.
Size dictates to stone, but you're in control.
Are you rock or pebble? Will you hold or roll?

MANLY GRANT
Rhymes for the Land

Andy returned the book to his cabin and I could hear him cleaning up inside, leaving me alone to think over all I had learned.

I now knew the essence of Spirit of the Squirrel. Worthwhile work, which meant three things:

—

Important
Leading to shared goals
Value-driven

—

As I watched evening slowly slide across Andy's clearing, I thought about how different the factory would be if Spirit of the Squirrel guided every team member.

Soon we were closing the cabin and heading back to Walton.

Once on the highway I saw again the specter of fifteen hundred families dependent upon how well I understood and applied Andy's lessons. And I didn't know it would feel worse, much worse, when I started to put names and faces to the people depending upon me.

When Andy dropped me back at the plant I handed him his extra helmet and asked, "You said it was a leader's job to impose respect for values. But that isn't going to work for the goals I set. How do I get people's support for my goals?"

"Easy question. Complex answer," said Andy as he turned off the Harley. "The closer you get to Gung Ho, the higher the trust level will be. That's what you need. Trust. As mutual trust rises, support for goals will increase."

"It's going to be tough getting anyone around this place to trust management," I said ruefully.

"Tough, but not impossible," said Andy. "I discovered I couldn't order people to support the goals I set. I could insist they respect certain values, but I couldn't make people commit to the goals. All I could do was tell them how they would benefit and invite them to join me."

"I can see why it took you five years to Gung Ho the department."

"Yeah, it didn't happen overnight. You have to give people time. And, as I said, you have to be willing to explain why the goals are important and honestly show how people benefit. Burn this into your mind in capital letters: TELL THE TRUTH.

"In court you have to swear 'to tell the truth, the whole truth, and nothing but the truth.' That's what we're talking about here and it's a tall order."

After a pause he added, "It goes beyond walk your talk. You've got to have honest talk to start with."

Andy went on to say that telling the truth and nothing but the truth was one thing. Telling the whole truth was quite another.

"Managers keep control by pretending information is sensitive and withholding it. It's great for power trips but it doesn't lead to trust. If you want your team to be Gung Ho, you have to tell the whole truth, and that means information belongs to everyone."

I was to learn living what I preached was tough. Preaching an honest message in the first place was a harder test. In tough situations it was difficult not to shade things by either withholding information, keeping my opinions to myself, or sugarcoating.

"I'll tell the truth," I promised. "What else can I do?"

"It all centers around trust. Along with total honesty, you have to put the well-being of your team members first. In the finishing department we have a five-point constitution. The first point is to protect the health, safety, and well-being of every person in the department," said Andy.

"That's interesting. At head office we always put making a profit first. Providing a return to shareholders."

"Ah, yes. Head office. Home of the skunks," laughed Andy. "Profit didn't even make it onto our five-point list. Nor did anything even close to rate of return on investment. I figure if you're doing the basics right, all the rest of that stuff will follow right along."

"It must, Andy. At head office we assigned fourteen percent of revenues to cover finishing costs. Based on how far you're below budget, you're making us buckets of money. That department of yours is a gold mine!"

"It wasn't always. I used to try to run my department from accounting reports. I was obsessed with our scrap ratio and such things as an overtime-to-material cost analysis report. I can't even remember what that was supposed to be all about now. Don't get me wrong. Accounting reports contain valuable information and you have to know what's going on. And you have to share it with the team. You've seen the charts and number boards up all over my department. But I discovered you have to go beyond the numbers. You have to see work as more than just units."

Andy again paused before giving me an important message: "Running a business from numbers is like playing basketball while watching the scoreboard instead of the ball. Look after the basics if you want success, and the first basic is the team."

Andy threw his leg back over his motorcycle, but I wasn't ready to let him go yet. I still had a couple of questions and I needed the answers.

"What about customers? Why weren't they first in your constitution?" I asked Andy.

"Customers came right after the team members. The *work* of an organization is to look after customers, but the *reason* the organization exists in the first place is to serve the people who work there, as well as the community they live in.

"There are lots of things you need to do to build trust but I have given you the two most important. Honesty and putting team members first. Do that and the rest will follow along easily."

"Getting support isn't going to happen overnight," I observed, as much to myself as to Andy.

"It's not. There's a fast way though. It's called fear. Frightened people will seize on to a rescue plan. But their support can evaporate just as fast. I don't think that's the way to begin, even though our time is short."

"I agree," I said. "So, where do I start?"

"I don't know," Andy replied. "I began with six people. We met for a beer after work twice a week and talked. When they understood the Spirit of the Squirrel and were excited, we brought in a couple more. We just kept expanding. With the time you've got though... who knows?"

I suspected Andy really had a pretty good idea of where I should start. I also guessed it must be one of those things in life that was better if you worked it out yourself, and Andy judged me able to do so.

"Okay," I said. "I'll work on that. When do I learn the Way of the Beaver?"

"First big rain," said Andy as his Harley roared back to life. "The Way of the Beaver comes with the first big rain. Up here that's usually about mid-September."

"Gung Ho, friend," he boomed out over the bike's rumble as he pulled away.

"Gung Ho, friend," I called after him.

Middle of September. That gave me about two weeks to get going on Spirit of the Squirrel. No problem, I told myself as I opened my car door. Two weeks was probably perfect.

The next morning was day three. At the end of my first day, I figured I was in big trouble. Day two brought hope. I wondered where day three would lead as I entered my office. It was early. I sat alone at my desk with poster board and crayons.

I soon had a poster to hang over my desk, decorated with a very fine squirrel drawing, if I do say so myself. It read:

SPIRIT OF THE SQUIRREL:
WORTHWHILE WORK

1. Knowing we make the world a better place.
2. Everyone works toward a shared goal.
3. Values guide all plans, decisions, and actions.

My Division Managers had departed en masse yesterday and this morning they arrived en masse. I sent word I'd meet with them in ten minutes.

From the cafeteria I ordered coffee. "Double caffeine. Brew it strong," I told the cook. I needed these people alert.

When they were settled in I began talking about the difference our products made to customers. As I talked I sensed small scratches of pride were opening up. Nothing major, mind you. But eyes remained open.

My ending also caught their attention.

"I like to think I know what this company is all about. However, I'd like to hear what you think. I want you to get your thoughts organized on three issues: Why are we here? What are our goals? What values will guide us? We'll meet back here tomorrow morning. I look forward to hearing your ideas."

At the suggestion that they contribute their own thoughts, looks ranging from acute heartburn to panic swept through the room. I just smiled and ended the meeting.

Frankly, I enjoyed watching them squirm. Had I known how quickly I'd be squirming myself, I would have felt more compassion.

The call came at noon. Old Man Morris was on the line and he wasn't happy. The figures for Walton Works #2 didn't look good. What was I going to do about it? At some point the plant would have to be closed if I didn't shape up.

I didn't miss the message. It was I who had to shape up. I'd been on the job two and a half days and I owned the problem.

"How long have I got?"

"I expect results by Christmas. That's four months. I think that's more than reasonable."

I swear I could hear Old Man Morris chuckling long after I'd hung up.

I shuffled out to Andy's motorcycle at shift change and gave him the news.

"I told you my wife said I was still mad from seeing those Saturday movies. Remember?"

"So?"

"Well, that may be. But I also learned something. The Indians may have lost every week, but by noon the next Saturday we were ready for another fight. Old Man Morris may have knocked us down but we have to be ready to fight again by Saturday."

"Andy, we don't have time. We can fight, but we can't win in four months."

"Well, we'll just have to get more time."

"Old Man Morris give me more time to look good? Forget it!"

"Four months. That brings us to year end. I can probably get us until next August. That's a year. We'll just have to do it in a year," said Andy.

"How can you get us until August?" I questioned. My voice clearly said, just who do you think you are? But Andy didn't take offense. He only smiled and said, "I've got an idea. Trust me?"

"It's not as if I had anything to lose," I replied and tried to give him a smile in return. "Gung Ho, friend?"

"Gung Ho, friend," he said giving me the thumbs-up sign.

Again Andy departed without looking back. I stood there, watching his motorcycle, thinking, well, if I'm prepared to run this place based on squirrels, with beavers and geese still to come, why not trust a Department Head to beat Old Man Morris's influence with the Board?

Friday morning I took my post at the head of the table as my Division Managers filed in. Initial statements were evasive and brief. I was at my gentle, patient best, and eventually, with effort, some true feelings and ideas began to emerge. A little genuine pride did exist, but it was obvious it would be a while before people wore their hearts on their sleeves. There was minimal interest in setting goals for growth that would require a stretch and a real challenge. Discussing values aroused only mild interest.

Later on these same Division Managers were going to play an important role in Gung Ho'ing Walton Works #2. It would never have happened without their hard work and support. But that was in the future. A long way in the future.

I announced that starting Monday, we would begin meeting every day after lunch for one hour to discuss three issues: Why we were here, what we thought our long-term and short-term goals should be, and what values we'd honor. I had little doubt about a couple of goals and values I'd insist on, but first I wanted to see what they came up with.

Saturday Andy showed up at my office door at noon.

"Figured you might be here. Can't spend the whole weekend in the office. What do you want to do? Go to the movies and watch the cowboys win or spend the afternoon at the cabin?"

"I think I've seen the movie. Let's do the cabin."

And so began a tradition. Saturday afternoon at the cabin. I asked him how his idea for postponing the plant closedown beyond Christmas was coming along.

"Bad idea," he laughed. "But don't worry. I'm working on another one."

I wished I could take more comfort from his confidence. At the cabin we reviewed where we were and set out plans for the week ahead. On Wednesday we'd push the process down one level, from Division Managers to Department Heads. That would involve another fifty people. The next week we'd involve the lead hands, a further two hundred.

I asked Andy that afternoon why his grandfather had used the term "Gung Ho." It just didn't seem to fit with squirrels, beavers, and geese. "It doesn't," agreed Andy, "but it fit Grandfather. He served in World War I and his speech was peppered with military phrases and words. He told me *gung ho* was Chinese for 'working together' and the slogan of Carlson's Raiders during World War II." *

When I tried to find out more about the Way of the Beaver, Andy put on his stoic Indian face and intoned, "Way of Beaver come with first big rain." I decided it was his way of telling me I had more than enough to keep me busy, and he was right.

The next few days were full, frantic, and sometimes fun. I also had times of panic and nights of worry. I couldn't pass a playground without looking at the children and realizing that their fathers and mothers worked at the plant.

To combat the paralyzing effects of worry I toured the plant every morning and then crossed over to the building that contained the finishing department. There it was. A Gung Ho jewel. My talisman that proved it could be done, if only I had the talent to pull it off. If only I had the time.

In the afternoon I went from department to department in the main plant, dragging a Division Manager, meeting with workers, and trying, at Andy's suggestion, to call them team members.

---

* Led by Lieutenant Colonel Evans F. Carlson, the men of the Second Marine Raider Division were known for their enthusiasm, teamwork, and outstanding results. The unit was formed seven weeks after Pearl Harbor and its success documented in the book *Gung Ho!* by Lieutenant W. S. Le Francois. When the book was turned into a movie starring wartime screen idol Randolph Scott (with Robert Mitchum in a supporting role), the term "Gung Ho," to describe boundless enthusiasm, energy, and dedication applied to some task, was firmly entrenched in our language.

My job, in these meetings, was to point out why Walton Works #2 made the world a better place. They didn't buy it all the first time. But they listened, and I opened every meeting by repeating the same message.

Once they understood I really wanted to talk about goals to be set jointly, not ones imposed by me or by Division Managers or head office, they began to open up. The cork had been in the bottle so long that, once loosened, it popped. But like the Division Managers, their focus wasn't on what they might do. Rather it was on what they wanted the company to do. It would take a while before they began to see themselves and the company as one and the same entity.

The interesting thing was, as they began to participate in goal setting, they became more receptive to my message that their work made a difference. That they were important. Goal setting, and understanding the true meaning of our work, notched up in tandem, one step at a time.

I had trouble getting discussion going concerning values. Andy said this was to be expected. Values were personal, as well as corporate, and people didn't talk easily about personal things. Be patient, he said; it will come.

It was a slow process though. In two weeks I felt there was a change in attitude, but the difference was small and

I knew it was fragile. Whatever the Way of the Beaver and Gift of the Goose might be, they would need to be powerful stuff if the plant was still to be open after New Year's Day.

"A year," Andy protested when I worried about how slowly we were progressing. "Don't forget I'm working on a year."

"Sorry. I forgot. A year. But even then. . ."

"Then we go out with our heads held high. But I'm betting on a year, and I'm betting we pull it off."

Some days I figured Andy must have gone to the movies every Saturday thinking, "This week the Indians are going to win. This week, for sure, the cowboys lose." I valued his optimism. But it was an optimism I found tough to share.

By this time I'd told my Division Managers the meaning of the Spirit of the Squirrel poster, although I hadn't yet told them about my source, or my final goal of Gung Ho. These Division Managers were not ready to accept the idea someone in the plant might know better than they how to run the shop floor.

But they were interested in what I was attempting, and together we had moved the process out into the whole plant, with the exception of the finishing department. I'd taken that department on myself when its Division Manager departed. I met with the finishing department, told them what we were up to, and swore them to secrecy.

"Interdepartment rivalry could kill this whole thing before we even get started. I want you people to lie low for now." The finishing department took the pledge.

I too had taken a pledge. Right in the plant I had 150 team members who already knew far more than I did about Gung Ho, but I'd promised Andy not to pry. It was important, he said, to follow the process in an orderly fashion.

And so I worked at instilling the Spirit of the Squirrel: worthwhile work. First, understanding that Walton Works #2 made the world a better place. Second, working toward a shared goal. And third, ensuring that values guided all plans, decisions, and actions.

One of my most difficult battles was opening up the flow of information. At this point I was only trying to put some basic stuff in the hands of Department Managers. You'd think I was trying to give away state military secrets to the enemy, judging from the reaction and roadblocks. But I was determined, and after I started mumbling about severance packages, a little information began to trickle out of the Division Managers' hands. I admit, using a threat wasn't the best way to get support. But I wasn't perfect then and I'm not now. Today though, I do try harder to be aware of what I'm really doing, and to respect others.

The following Saturday Andy made a great show of examining the sky before we left for the cabin.

Then, taking a leaf, he crumbled it in his hand and threw the pieces up in the air where the breeze carried them a short distance. Andy watched the crumbled bits hit the ground, and after a short, but very official-sounding chant he announced, "Heavy rainstorm come. Trip canceled. Way of the Beaver tomorrow."

The twinkle in his eye and his exaggerated parody of Saturday matinee Indianspeak should have alerted me, but I walked right into it.

"You can tell a storm is coming from that clear sky and crumbled leaves?"

"That, plus magic-box weather spirit," asserted Andy. "Powerful medicine."

Glancing skyward Andy held his arms out wide as if to embrace the heavens and intoned, "Learn name of weather spirit and become seer of future."

"Yes?" I encouraged expectantly.

"Willard Scott. TV Two. Seven A.M. Followed by Sandy, local weather lady. Very reliable. Powerful medicine. As for the leaves? Great show for tourists and gullible bosses."

Instant thoughts of how I might get back at Andy flashed through my mind, but I smiled my sweetest smile to show I could take a joke.

But the Way of the Beaver beckoned. Andy had promised I'd learn Grandfather's Way of the Beaver, come the first big rain.

The magic-box forecasters were indeed powerful medicine. The rain began at 3:00 P.M. and for six hours sheets of water poured down. The river beside the plant turned from a placid, slow-moving mass into a turbulent and tumbling torrent. Apparently rains like this came every September.

By the time I left church at noon the next day the sky had cleared and a warm sun shone on a soggy Walton. My spirits weren't dampened though. We had had the big rain. The Way of the Beaver was to follow.

Andy's Episcopalian service had let out ten minutes before my Presbyterian one ended, and he was out front waiting for me.

"Gung Ho, friend," he greeted me as I came scurrying down the walk and clambered up on the motorcycle.

"Gung Ho, friend," I replied as I buckled my helmet and threw my arms around Andy. "Let's vamoose."

Our destination turned out to be the cabin and Andy insisted on lunch. "We've the whole afternoon for Way of the Beaver."

"Andy, we're talking about the future of fifteen hundred people plus the whole town of Walton."

"Eat first. Way of the Beaver second."

Guilt and/or intimidation wasn't going to get me any-where. I ate my sandwich as suggested and took comfort in the thought that I'd soon have the next piece of the puzzle. The next key to saving Walton Works #2.

"I suppose you'll be having your nap in the hammock as usual after lunch," I accused.

"Most assuredly not. We have work to do. It's time we were off."

And off we were. Through the woods behind the cabin at a brisk pace. Down the path we soon came to an old abandoned logging road, which we followed for about a mile. Then we turned right, down another path, which led to the edge of a pond circled by a narrow trail.

The rain had filled the pond beyond capacity. Trees were standing in the water. In several spots the trail was washed out. On the far side we came upon a large tree in which, ten feet up, I could see several boards anchored between two substantial branches and the trunk. A homemade ladder gave access.

"Here we are," said Andy. "Up we go."

We had a perfect perch to see a beaver dam, damaged by the heavy rain. Water was spilling out over a fifteen-foot section that had lost its top two feet of twigs, trees, and mud. New tree branches were already anchored in the old base.

We sat down cross-legged and Andy handed me binoculars.

"Normally beavers do dam maintenance at night, but this break is major. They'll be working on it in daylight. That's their lodge over there."

"You mean that pile of sticks?"

"That's it. The entrance is underwater. The floor inside is above water level but the water protects the doorway. Even if we began ripping away at the outside they could slip out underwater and get away. It's critical they control the water level."

"Spirit of the Squirrel," I observed.

"Exactly. But this is a more complex society and community than that of squirrels. There's a lot more going on here, and more to learn."

We sat quietly and waited. I found myself thinking how much was riding on the next few hours. If I was ever inclined to forget the time left, Old Man Morris was there to keep me posted on the calendar.

"Hear you've been having a lot of feel-good meetings," he'd grumped when he called Friday. "If you spent the time working you might save that plant. Can't meet your way to success. Have to work your way there. But go ahead. Have your meetings. Christmas is coming."

I knew the Christmas present he had in mind for me, and I was determined to spoil his fun. But time was on his side. Andy continued to claim he had a plan. Without it we had three and a half months to do the impossible.

A tug on my sleeve brought me back. A brown head, fur slick with water, had broken the surface. A telltale ripple angled out behind as the beaver started to move. Three other heads popped up.

Andy spoke quietly. "The Spirit of the Squirrel leads to Gung Ho only when it is matched with Way of the Beaver."

It was easy to see why the phrase "busy as a beaver" was part of our language. Like the squirrels, they seemed tireless. Luckily the high water put many trees within easy reach. These they cut down with their teeth, a noisy process I discovered, and then dragged them through the water to the repair site. Holding a branch in their teeth, they dove down or pulled a tree trunk up, looking for a place to anchor it. Once or twice the current washed a hard-won branch over the dam. It was an inconvenience the beavers had learned to deal with. They headed right back for another.

I watched, fascinated by the drive and energy that sustained them. Again Andy spoke quietly. "The Way of the Beaver answers the question: Who is in charge here?"

A boss beaver? It wasn't readily apparent which beaver was senior. After half an hour I was no wiser. Exactly what pattern was being followed was a mystery. I'd just think I'd discovered one and it ended. Finally I admitted defeat.

"I'm sorry, Andy. I can't tell. It doesn't look like anyone's in charge," I said softly.

"And if no one's in charge, who tells each beaver what to do next and how to do it?" prompted Andy.

"I guess they tell themselves," I ventured.

"You've got it!" Andy exclaimed with such enthusiasm that a loud warning crack of a beaver's tail whacking the water rang out and four beavers plunged below the surface.

"Oops. Got carried away," said Andy in a normal voice. "But that's okay. They'll be down for a couple of minutes. Give us a chance to talk instead of whisper."

"The Way of the Beaver is being your own boss?" I questioned Andy.

By way of answering, Andy reached in his backpack and withdrew a carving I recognized immediately. It was an Andrew Payton beaver. Propped up by the tail, the beaver stood on hind legs, a stick between its teeth held in place by front paws. Again the detail was superb.

I didn't stop to admire the carving but flipped it over, skipped the name, the date, and read the second secret:

—

The Way of the Beaver:
In control of achieving the goal

—

Andy said, "Each beaver has a large measure of control over its own destiny. They decide how the work is going to be done. They operate like independent contractors."

There it was. The Way of the Beaver. If I had any question as to exactly what it meant, Andy quickly set me straight.

"If everybody has the Spirit of the Squirrel, but management makes the workers do everything by management's book, that organization won't be Gung Ho. Chances are, management's way won't be the workers' way, and so the workers won't be able to produce as well. Besides, the workers' way will likely be better. Much better. Nothing kills Gung Ho faster than narrow-minded and likely mean-spirited management, chipping away at workers' self-esteem by insisting things be done the bosses' way."

"Ouch. That sounds just like Walton Works #2!"

"It does, doesn't it?" said Andy with characteristic directness. "These beavers don't achieve engineering marvels because some other beaver is ordering them around. It's up to each of them how the dam gets repaired. If they want to work at one end, fine. If they want to bring small branches, that's great. They exercise their own best judgment.

"It is important to understand that these beavers do what they do because they decide to. Not because they've been ordered to. The Way of the Beaver means team members must control achieving their goal. Grandfather said it was doing right work the right way."

"That doesn't sound like Walton Works #2 this time."

"No, it doesn't. Those people aren't really team members. They're workers—their orders are to follow orders. Not very interesting. Not fulfilling. But once you begin to let employees have a real say in the way things are done, and they accept the challenge, you soon won't recognize the place."

"Don't I get a say in where we're going?" I wondered. "Sounds to me like you're telling me to turn the factory over to the workers, except we call them team members, and that's it."

"Not at all. Your job as General Manager is the same as any true leader's. Let people know why the work is worthwhile. Decide where you're going. Make sure the team shares the goal. Help set values. Get the resources in place. Hold the rule makers in check. Ensure you've got the support you need both inside and outside the organization. Keep your eye on the future to ward off trouble and be ready to change direction.

"As for the team? You have to let the people who really do the work do the work. It's your job as leader to know where the plant is going. It's the team members' job to get you there."

I thought Andy might be finished, but he went on and gave me a lesson that was to be one of the most important and useful I learned that day.

"By setting the key goals and values, you define the playing field and the rules of the game. You decide who plays what position. Then you have to get off the field and let the players move the ball.

"The goals and values are like sidelines. The players have to know that as long as they follow the rules they can go anywhere within the lines. And they have to know that when the ball is in play you'll keep off the field.

"If you want your people to take charge, they have to be free to do it, and freedom comes from knowing exactly what territory is yours. Knowing how far you can go before you're out of bounds has to be matched with knowing the boss isn't about to step in and take over."

"It's a bit of a paradox," I said. "When I set limits on how far people can go I also give them the freedom to move."

"When you say how far they can go, what you're really saying is how far you'll go," replied Andy. "Grandfather said the Great Spirit painted a picture in the beavers' head of what a perfect dam looked like, gave them a stream and some trees, and then put them in charge by leaving them alone."

After a pause I said, "If everybody made decisions like those beavers, going their own way, even if goals and values do set limits, it could be quite a mess."

"If people were beavers it would be," said Andy. "But we're not. Several things distinguish us from other animals. Thumbs, language, and—far, far more than any other species—we work together to achieve our goals. And remember, with Spirit of the Squirrel we've already established well-understood and shared goals. There may be some mavericks, and they're not all bad if you don't have too many, but you'll find people will naturally work together.

"The real secret of successful management is discovering what people do naturally and then figuring out how to adapt the organization to take advantage of natural behavior. Too many managers go at it the other way around."

"It may be natural, but I have the feeling it's still going to be tough," I said.

"It is. It won't be easy for you. It's tough to be boss without being bossy. You need high self-esteem. It will be tougher for the team members than you though."

"How's that? They wind up with more control. How can that be tough? Isn't that what they want?" I asked.

"That's what most of them want and they'll respond in time. But change is hard. They may not like the way things are run now but they know how to cope. Old familiar problems are more comfortable than new strange ones."

The beavers began to surface on the far side of the pond. We fell silent and watched them go back to work. Working the Way of the Beaver: each in control of achieving the goal. Right work being done the right way.

A short while later something alerted one of them to danger and with a warning crack of its tail down it went, followed promptly by the others.

"We may as well be on our way," said Andy. "We can continue the discussion as we walk back."

We wrapped the beaver carving in its protective cover and stored it in Andy's backpack. I was sorry to leave, but Andy assured me we could return. "It will have to be in the early evening though. You need a dam break to force them out in midday."

After we had skirted the pond and were back on the logging road, Andy continued the lesson.

"Grandfather said:

—

The Way of the Beaver Fulfills God's Plan for the Beaver.

—

I thought about this as we walked along. "That's interesting. Your grandfather said the Spirit of the Squirrel

GUNG HO!

fulfilled God's plan for the forest, and now the Way of the Beaver fulfills His plan for the beaver."

"The first addresses the needs of society," replied Andy. "The second, the needs of the individual.

"The Way of the Beaver describes the individual's relationship to the organization. And once you know that, you really know the other side as well. The organization's relationship to the individual."

"Which is?" I prompted.

"Think about it. How is each beaver treated by the others?"

"Pretty good, I guess."

"Meaning?"

"Well, they don't seem to bite or fight. They're not like the squirrels. One squirrel always seems to be chasing off another. You'd think there wasn't enough seed for everyone the way they go at each other."

"Only thing worse than one bossy boss is everyone wanting to be boss," said Andy. "What else? Do they mess with another beaver's work?"

"No. If one beaver puts a branch in place the others leave it."

"Right again," said Andy. "Beavers respect each other. You can't be in control if everything you do gets ripped apart. And one beaver doesn't hide a good tree from the other beavers. They all have access to what's available to get the job done and that includes full, accurate, and

[**74**]

up-to-the-minute information on everything. No secrets. The rest of the organization has to support you if you're going to take control of your own work."

Then Andy said, "Remember: *People who are truly in control work for organizations that value them as persons. Their thoughts, feelings, needs, and dreams are respected, listened to, and acted upon.*"

Both of us walked in silence while I considered this. The Way of the Beaver covered the relationship of an individual and an organization from both sides. The first side was the individual taking charge. Being in control of achieving the goal. The second side was an organization that allowed and encouraged individuals to do so. And when that happened, their thoughts, feelings, needs, and dreams were respected, listened to, and acted upon.

"It's really a Golden Rule for management, isn't it?" I said.

"I'd never thought of it that way, but you're right. You don't have to go any further than valuing individuals as persons. Do that and you've got it all."

I gave a short laugh.

"What's so funny?" Andy asked with surprise.

"Sorry. No disrespect to your grandfather. I was just thinking how different it is from Old Man Morris's Golden Rule. He says: 'He who has the gold makes the rules.'"

"Sounds like him," said Andy. "As I told you before, it takes a lot of self-esteem to be boss without being bossy. I can't think he holds himself in very high regard."

I'd never thought about it, but I realized Andy must be right. Old Man Morris could be up only when others were down.

We had reached a spot on the old logging road where the rainstorm had washed over, leaving a rut of soggy mud. Andy helped me across as he had on the way out.

"We've talked about two sides to Way of the Beaver. There are really three. It's more like a triangle than a coin. The third side is that beavers have work they can do. They build dams with trees and mud. They couldn't be in control of achieving the goal if they were expected to build a concrete dam. The Way of the Beaver requires work that's possible. Grandfather said you had to give people work they can do. You can't expect to achieve production beyond their reasonable capacity or skills beyond their training."

"That's understandable."

"Ha," snorted Andy. "It might be to you, but you'll want to take a look at what's actually happening back at the factory. The production norms sometimes expect ten hours of output for eight hours of time and pay. No one, and no department, has achieved some of those numbers since some boob from head office posted them ten years ago. But they're still up there on the wall, unchanged."

"I'll deal with that," I announced.

Andy, however, was on a roll and wasn't about to be slowed down.

"The plant has the reverse problem too. Matter of fact, it's worse. Much worse. We've got production norms that can be met by noon on any bad day you care to mention. When you undershoot, you won't make people happy. You insult them," said Andy, kicking a soft lump of dirt into a spray of mud to emphasize his point.

"I thought they'd be glad to goof off," I said.

"On the surface they are, but deep down, don't you believe it. Nothing drains self-esteem faster than knowing you're ripping off the system. Not earning your pay. That's when you get big-shot talk, but it doesn't help heal the hurt. If people can't do a fair day's work for a fair day's pay, you demean them. They won't easily forgive that."

"That's interesting. I remember my father said that paying his fair share of taxes was part of having a good day. I've never heard anybody else single out paying taxes as the mark of having a good day. But he was right. I've always been proud to be a taxpayer. A contributor."

"Nothing demeans faster than getting something for nothing. It's the same when you don't let people contribute, perform up to their capacity," agreed Andy.

"It's the same story for skill levels," he cautioned. "Every time you expect work from people who aren't trained for it, you sabotage Gung Ho. Take a look at your training budget! I spend more on groceries in a month than the whole plant does on skill training or upgrading in a year.

"When those new presses went into H Section three years ago, they were lucky to get shop manuals for the computer controls, much less any training. And then the Division Manager wondered why productivity went down. The wonder is it didn't go to zero."

"So what's the answer?" I asked. "Even if we do proper training, apparently I'll insult people when I expect too little. And you say demanding too much is near as bad. How do I find the middle?"

"The answer isn't having expectations bang in the middle," said Andy. "Just asking people to do what they are able to do easily won't give people the feeling of accomplishment they need to be Gung Ho. You have to stretch them. Give them work that demands their best and allows them to learn and move ahead into uncharted territory."

Andy's advice matched my own experience.

"That makes sense. I'm always happiest when I've got a challenging problem to work on," I replied. "Yet one I believe I can do. Like right now. Gung Ho'ing our factory. I feel more alive and excited now than I have for years."

"It's going to be a challenge all right. And I believe you can do it. Provided they don't close us down first. In life you've got to be ready for the cowboys to win again. Especially when you don't get to write the script."

Andy had brought reality to the excitement I'd been feeling. It was a sobering fact. Our time was limited.

At that very moment, as if the forest could read my thoughts, it sent me the same message.

We had just turned from the logging road onto the cabin's path when a large gray bird took flight with a mournful moan.

"What's that?" I asked as Andy stopped to watch the bird glide along the path with slow rhythmic beats of giant wings and then disappear to the left.

"Owl. A gray owl."

"I thought owls gave a friendly *whoo.* That one sounds as if he's carrying all the cares of the world," I said.

"He may be," Andy replied soberly. "The Kwakiutl Indians believed an owl called your name when you died."

"Margaret Craven," I said, suddenly remembering the name of an author whose novel, *I Heard the Owl Call My Name,* I'd read years ago. It was about an Indian band living by the ocean in British Columbia. Obviously Andy remembered the author's name as well.

"Wonderful book," he said as he started off down the path again. "And when you're an Indian it gives you a whole new respect for owls."

Then he added very seriously, "The day Grandfather died, he finished carving an owl. I think the owl waited for him to complete it."

Andy, I knew, sang in the choir on Sunday and led a Bible study for teenagers on Tuesday evenings. At the same time he also retained respect for his own traditions and the teachings that had guided the Longclaw family for many generations.

We completed the walk back to the cabin with little further talk. In addition to thinking about the ominous appearance of the owl and reviewing what I'd been told, I was planning a new poster. I figured I could draw a pretty good beaver right on the top.

WAY OF THE BEAVER:
IN CONTROL OF ACHIEVING THE GOAL

1. A playing field with clearly marked territory.
2. Thoughts, feelings, needs, and dreams are respected, listened to, and acted upon.
3. Able but challenged.

All I had to do was actually make it happen in fourteen weeks! I wondered if Gift of the Goose would help speed things up. Back on the cabin porch, I asked Andy.

"Big help," he said with a nod. "But Gift of the Goose comes first week of November, give or take a week."

"Why so long?" I groaned.

"The geese don't come down from Canada until then," he said with a touch of wonder in his voice, leaving unsaid, "Don't city people know anything?"

"Great. No geese until November," I grumbled. "Eight weeks before D-Day."

"A year. I'm working on a year."

"And if not," I said looking at him with a smile, and we said in unison, "Heads held high!"

Andy knew I was worried the owl was about to call the name of Walton Works #2. I wasn't my usual happy self as we rode back to town.

"We won't win unless *you* believe we can," he said when he dropped me off.

"We can win, Andy. It's the time. We don't have the time. We've got the Spirit of the Squirrel and now you've given me the Way of the Beaver. But we don't have the time," I anguished.

"Attitude you can control, and your attitude will be reflected by everyone else. You go in looking like you do now and it's over. Remember, you're onstage. You have to give a performance. Lots of days when I was Gung Ho'ing the finishing department I didn't want to get out of bed, things were so awful. I was alone, no one cared, and I wondered why I cared. But I had to put on my best face and plunge right in every day."

"Why did you care, Andy?" I wondered.

"It's how I kept my sanity. My family was gone. I had to do something. If I thought about my own situation I'd have died too. I had to do something for others. Then, when Grandfather died, I realized I was his only grand-child and Gung Ho was all the two of us had to leave behind. If I couldn't leave my genes and DNA I could at least leave Gung Ho."

It was a pep talk that turned me around. Although Andy didn't say so, it was clear I was now part of that chain.

"Gotcha, Andy," I said as brightly as I could.
"Gung Ho, friend," he replied as he drove off.
"Gung Ho, friend," I called out.
As always Andy didn't look back.

Monday I woke up, looked at the sun coming up over the garden wall, and tested out a Bible verse that had been one of my mother's favorites: **This is the day which the Lord hath made; let us rejoice and be glad in it.** Louder, I told myself. At the top of my lungs I blasted it out again. There! That felt better. I decided I'd scared off any owl within a hundred miles.

By the time I hit the office I was primed and ready. Crayons and poster board were in hand. I had work to do before the Monday afternoon meeting.

When the meeting opened I plunged right in. "Today I want to add another agenda item: How are we going to make our goals happen?" I announced.

The Division Managers looked at me with anxious worry. I let my eyes roam around the table slowly before I spoke again. "You'll be glad to know I have a plan. A way of reaching our goals that's foolproof."

Glad doesn't tell the half of it. The danger was past. They had escaped being put on the spot. Tense shoulders relaxed. Creased brows unfurrowed. Then I zinged them. I know I shouldn't have enjoyed doing it, but I did.

"Here's my plan. I'm going to let each of you decide exactly what you're going to do, and how you're going to do it. You people know your departments far better than I. It would be foolish for me to try to tell you what to do," I said, pausing to let this sink in before I continued.

"I do have one suggestion though. Your team members know the shop floor, where work really happens, a hundred times better than you or I could ever hope to. Involve your team. Get their ideas and plans. Believe me, those ideas and plans will be far more productive than any we could come up with."

Consulting workers wasn't something these managers did naturally. Matter of fact, it wasn't something they did at all. Before they raised too many objections in their minds I plunged right into the Way of the Beaver.

"I've told you about Spirit of the Squirrel: worthwhile work based on understanding its true meaning, shared goals, and value-based plans, decisions, and actions. I know you thought that was off the wall, but I think you'll agree it's a good way of expressing a powerful management tool."

I could see several slight nods. At least I had their agreement and attention.

"Today I want to tell you about the Way of the Beaver. The Spirit of the Squirrel has value only when it's done the Way of the Beaver. Let me show you a poster I made this morning for my office wall."

I don't claim the managers were enthusiastic, or even keen. But they did listen with interest, and before the meeting ended they agreed to try consulting front line people. What this might mean in practice, who knew? But I figured I'd done about as well as I was going to. Give me six months, I might even get them on my side.

The next Saturday at our cabin planning session, Andy and I decided the time had come to tie Spirit of the Squirrel and Way of the Beaver into the goal of Gung Ho. Monday afternoon the seventeen Division Managers would be taken on a tour of the finishing department.

To this day I'm astonished at what was happening—or rather not happening—at Walton Works #2. Here these seventeen Division Managers sat, right on top of the most productive department in our entire system, running the most unproductive departments, and yet they paid scant, if any, attention to it. Certainly they never tried to find out what was going on, what lessons they might learn and apply to their own departments.

"I bet if you weren't an Indian they'd be all over your department," I said one time to Andy.

"I don't know," said Andy dubiously. "I'd be the last to claim that being Indian gives a lot of instant credibility with the rest of the world when it comes to management. But I doubt those Division Managers get far enough outside the glare of their own brilliance and self-importance to even notice me, much less that I'm Indian."

Andy may have been right. The Division Managers saw little beyond the footlights of the executive office. Pity their light wasn't bright enough to shine as far as the finishing department!

To help center the spotlight we decided the time had come to give them a jolt of reality. With luck, the promise of Gung Ho would keep fear to a minimum while reality focused attention. I was going to have to walk a fine line.

"I've got good news and bad news for you today," I began the Monday meeting. "First, the bad."

I had their attention. Heads lifted and looked at me expectantly.

"Unless we show a significant improvement in productivity by year end, enough to put this plant operating in the black under the new cost-accounting policies, head office has decided to close us down."

Shock registered on every face. Then suddenly, seventeen voices all began asking questions and clamoring for attention at once. I held up my hand and they fell silent.

"I also said I have some good news. All we have to do to save this plant and our jobs is bring up our productivity to match the other plants in our system. We're not being asked to do something extraordinary. Others are doing it and we can too. Our equipment is as good, our wage rates compare favorably. We have a people problem and we have to solve it by Christmas or we're gone."

Protests, complaints, justifications, and cries of unfair and comments on the general stupidity of head office rang out. I let them have a few minutes to vent. I again held up my hand for silence. The rumblings around the table died down.

"I have another piece of good news. At Walton Works #2 we have the most productive department in our whole system. The finishing department. All we need do is learn what they are doing right, why they do it, how they do it, when they do it, and then put that to work in the rest of the plant."

That should perk them up. Their response? Noncommittal silence. I decided I'd take that as a good sign. Andy's optimism must have been catching! I gave another try.

"Best of all, we're already doing it," I announced. "We've been working on two of the three secrets responsible for the finishing department's success: Spirit of the Squirrel and Way of the Beaver. Did you know that?"

Silence and awkward shuffles.

"Have any of you actually been in the finishing department?"

Not a single person spoke up. The most productive department in thirty-two plants; seventeen Division Managers sitting right on top; not one of them had a clue what was going on!

Well, I'd enlighten them.

"The whole process is called Gung Ho. Everyone in the finishing department is Gung Ho and everybody at Walton Works #2 has to be Gung Ho by year end. It's that simple."

The plan had been to leave it there and then take the seventeen Division Managers to the finishing department. But I found myself continuing.

"I know our time is short. But we have five weeks of squirrels and beavers under our belts. We also have a choice. Head office thinks we're a worthless bunch of losers. They think we can't do it. They think Walton Works #2 is doomed. I think they're wrong. I think Old Man Morris is wrong. I think we can turn this place around and make all those paper pushers at head office eat their words!"

Andy had said fear could bring people together, but it was a dangerous way to go. As the managers faced reality, fear was held in check because there was another powerful motivator we'd both forgotten about: pride and a common enemy. Spirit of the Squirrel had given us a touch of pride. Head office writing us off provided a great common enemy. As soon as I said we could make the paper pushers at head office eat their words, I could sense a shift in the room. The possibility of seventeen individuals becoming one team opened.

Andy would guide the tour. I set out the rules. Questions would be limited to Spirit of the Squirrel and Way of the Beaver. The third pillar on which the department's success was built, Gift of the Goose, was off limits.

Second rule, after the tour we'd keep away from the finishing department. I explained my concerns about interdepartment rivalry. This they knew about. Seventeen heads nodded with understanding.

We walked across the parking lot to Building D and the finishing department. A trip seventeen of us had never made before. Andy met us outside. Behind him the door was firmly closed.

"I suppose Ms. Sinclair has been spouting off all that nonsense about squirrels and beavers," he opened. The others were surprised. I was shocked.

"It's a good thing you came over," he deadpanned. "I don't mean to be critical, but stress sometimes can get to people."

People nothing. He meant me!

"You'd better come back in the shop with me and see what the real world is like. The only way to keep those rats at their machines would be to chain them in place and the law won't let me do that."

About half the Division Managers looked puzzled. The other half were ready to vote for a chain law as a reasonable productivity-enhancement regulation.

"Watch your step," said Andy as he went toward the door. "The floor can be slippery and a couple of lights are burned out."

Andy had painted a picture not much different from the rest of our factory. The Division Managers knew what to expect. They stopped dead in their tracks as they went through the door. It was 30,000 square feet of splendor. The only jarring note was Andy's chuckle as he followed them in.

"Like I said, it's a rat's nest," Andy laughed. "But we've got plans to improve. There are lots of things we're going to do to make it better."

"This is more like an office than a factory," blurted out one amazed Division Manager.

"Why not?" replied Andy. "This is the office for everyone out here." Wide windows added natural light to the large lamps that flooded the shop. Green plants hung in baskets from pastel-painted walls, and much of the floor was carpeted. Carpeted!

The various pieces of equipment gleamed and glowed with fresh polish. All over the walls were the graphs and posters. The department's constitution was there too. And the people! Both men and women, about one hundred in all on the day shift, and each wore a bright red uniform shirt and gray slacks.

"We've been had," groaned one Division Manager, and the others laughed. I gave a deep sigh of relief. It wasn't the way I'd have done it. But I remembered Way of the Beaver: in control of achieving the goal. It sounded good in theory, but living with it would take some getting used to.

The Division Managers were impressed. The team members looked sharp, acted sharp, and the whole department was spotlessly clean. There was an intensity of purpose you could feel just watching people working.

While my seventeen executives were blown away with what they saw, I was amazed that this had existed under their noses for so long and they'd never even bothered to check it out.

Andy once told me being left alone was a major plus. "Having explosive paint, we had to have our own building. Being ignored by everyone, even our Division Manager, was a big help. If anyone had been on top of us we'd never have had the freedom to become Gung Ho in the first place." Frighteningly true.

"Any similarity between this department and the rest of the plant is purely coincidental," observed the Division Manager standing closest to Andy.

"It wasn't always like this," said Andy.

"When I first took over it was filthy in here. I used to fire people at the drop of a hat and ship second-rate product just to meet production schedules. Like the rest of this plant does now," he added unnecessarily. I guessed he was entitled though.

"I was miserable and everyone else was miserable. Then I learned about Gung Ho. That was important, but there was something even more important."

Andy had the attention of the Division Managers and at his last admission he had my attention as well. More important?

"I decided the reason I was so miserable was that our product was bad and the workers were so awful to deal with." Andy paused and looked quickly at each Division Manager in turn.

"It dawned on me they were miserable because I was a real pain to work for and the plant a horrible place to work. Nothing was going to change unless I changed."

Then he added, "Nothing is going to change in the rest of Walton Works #2 unless you, your department heads, and your lead hands change."

Andy's message hit home. I too had to change. I had to stop zinging Division Managers. How could I expect anything from them if I kept treating them the way I had been? I don't claim I was able to change in that instant but I began trying. As my mind rejoined the group, Andy was still talking.

"Change doesn't mean just getting rid of old habits. It means developing new habits to replace the old."

"Can you give us an example, Andy?" I asked, wondering what new habit I might take up to replace the way I sometimes treated Division Managers now. *Respect* came quickly to mind.

"Sure can," Andy answered. "Take huddle and the morning cheer. Our old habit was to shuffle into work unsure of what was going on but knowing survival meant head down and keep quiet. Now our new habit is huddle and the cheer. The old habit won't change until the new replaces it."

"You really have a huddle and a cheer?" a Division Manager asked.

"We do. I wanted a team. Good teams always have a game plan and some form of huddle to be sure the players know what the next play or set of plays will be. So every morning we have a huddle to go over the work for the day. At the end of huddle we reach out, pile our hands together, and give a victory yell."

As we walked around the floor we stopped at work stations, each of which had its own charts and graphs, and spoke with the team members. Several boasted of recent accomplishments. One had shaved seven minutes off a process time. Another had completed a statistical analysis of a tank's ability to maintain electroplating tolerances. A third had finished two days of preventive maintenance on a piece of equipment that was now ready to go back into production.

"Who decided to tear it down?" he was asked.

"I did," he replied. "Of course, I told the rest of the team at huddle what I'd decided."

Of course!

It was evident that everyone was enjoying their day at work. Whenever Andy spoke with a team member, the overall production targets for the day and the week were invariably mentioned. One Division Manager noted with considerable amazement that the workers all seemed to have up-to-the-minute "confidential" information.

"Right," agreed Andy. "Information is the gatekeeper to power. I want the team in charge, with the power to make decisions and make things happen. In this department there's no such thing as confidential information. Everybody has full open access to everything."

As we were about to leave I asked one of the Division Managers to pick a team member at random. "I've got a couple of questions I'd like to ask and I want you all to pay attention to the answers."

Andy looked startled. Well, let him. He'd opened with an introduction that wasn't part of our plan. I'd provide the unscripted ending.

The team member was happy to visit. "Good to have you folks here," he said with a wave of his hand in greeting.

"Everyone in this department looks like they're working hard. Why's that?" I began.

"It's not hard work when you're enjoying it," the middle-aged man replied. "I used to work hard at my last job. I've been here five years and it doesn't seem like hard work at all."

"What's the difference between here and the last place you worked?"

"Gung Ho," laughed the man. "Andy says we all have to be Gung Ho. It's a great idea. This is the only place I've ever worked where I really know what's going on and what happens to the product I work on."

"Sounds good. Anything else?'

The man thought for a moment and then replied. "Several things. For one, I'm not treated like a piece of machinery. When we changed over the paint line last year I helped design my area with the engineers.

"Twenty of us have this work area and we run it like our own business. We're responsible for quality, on-time delivery, and looking after our customers. How we do it is mostly up to us. Last place I worked I made a suggestion once and the foreman said, 'I'll tell you what to do. You do it the way I tell you.' Those were his words."

At that moment a horn sounded and a loudspeaker announced, "Shipping **M317** at **100,** on time for **$12,750**."

A cheer went up from the shop floor. Someone rang a cowbell! It lasted perhaps five or six seconds. The Division Managers were startled.

"What was that?" I asked on behalf of everyone.

"That," said the man, "was exactly what I was about to tell you. The single biggest difference between this department and any other place I know of is the constant flow of positive, happy things that happen. That cheer was because we shipped job **M317** on time. It was **100** percent perfect and the plant took in **$12,750** of revenue.

"Cheering sales is only part of it. The best part is cheering people. We've always got some sort of contest going on. We have several monthly awards, and it's a rare day Andy doesn't drop by to cheer me on. Sometimes it's as simple as picking up a piece of work and saying how nice it looks. Then several times a week it will be someone's birthday, so we'll have a cake and sing at coffee break. I know it's corny, but I love it on my birthday."

He stopped talking but we could all tell he had something more to say. It was simple and to the point.

"The last place, **I HAD** to go to work. Here I **GET** to go to work."

Along with seventeen Division Managers I filed out of the finishing department thinking about what we'd just heard, and what would happen if the rest of our plant felt this way.

That week was the most productive yet for spreading the Spirit of the Squirrel and Way of the Beaver. But it wasn't going to happen in a week, or a month, or even by year end. We were behind too big a mountain of inertia and distrust to dig our way through quickly. By next summer we might have a chance. At year end, we were going to be toast.

Three things kept us going. The first was the drive to prove head office wrong. It was elemental in its motivating power. The second was the idea of "heads held high," which I'd initiated with the Division Managers. The third was a miracle. We didn't have a miracle. But we prayed for one.

The following week didn't go as well. I had a tough time keeping my attitude positive. People knew our ship was sinking, and they were fighting over which seat was theirs for the ride to the bottom! Battles for turf control were breaking out between divisions and even within departments.

"Not surprising," Andy assured me. We were at his cabin. Summer shirts had given way to fall jackets. "Tradition around the plant says everybody has well-defined rights and territory. Not much about responsibility, mind you, but we're big on rights and territory. You've started people looking at things differently and their natural instinct is to put what they can within their own boundary.

"You put an old dog in a new yard and first thing they do is piss on the fence posts to mark out their territory. All we're seeing is fence post pissing. Bound to happen."

Then he added, "People are no different from dogs that way. Grandfather said it was difficult for small-pie families to eat at the same table with large-pie folk."

"Which means?"

"Which means some people are small-pie people. They spend their whole lives convinced there is only so much pie to go around. They sit down at the table and start to fight over who gets what, worried someone else is getting more than their share. They love boundaries and fence posts to protect their territory.

"Big-pie people assume there's lots for everybody. More than enough. They've got an expanding pie. They trust anyone in the family to divide up the pie. No need for fences when the field is bigger than everyone could possibly need."

"And you're saying Walton Works #2 is filled with small-pie people?"

"I am. And Gung Ho people are big-pie people. When you start small-pie people thinking there may be extra pie, it's no wonder turf battles break out."

"We must be making progress, then. Lots of progress. We've sure spawned a crop of squabbles," I said.

"Can't be helped," Andy assured me. "And it's going to continue until they realize that with territory comes responsibility and there's more than enough of both for everyone."

Andy and I formulated our plan for the coming week, as we did every Saturday, and on Monday I plunged back in. Everyone in Walton Works #2 had been involved in the process for some time now. The Spirit of the Squirrel was at work and pride was building.

Matching work to ability, yet providing a challenge for team members, was slowly starting to happen. Everyone agreed it was a great idea. It was just going to take time to juggle people and workloads to make the match.

When we were at the cabin Andy had given me some more of Grandfather's wisdom. This time it was on challenging team members.

"Grandfather said, 'Canvas and wood make a boat. Only rapids can make a canoe.'"

I had looked quizzically at Andy. My city background didn't always prepare me to follow Grandfather's teachings without some help.

"Until you test a canoe in whitewater, you don't really know what you've got. You don't know how strong it is or how well it will handle a load. Once tested, once successful, though, its value and worthiness soar. Valuable, productive, worthy people are those who have been successfully tested. You know it and they know it."

Outside help had been hired to give us a hand designing a learning program that would bolster missing skill levels, prepare team members for the next step in their careers, and provide some ongoing general education as well. I enrolled in a Tuesday evening blueprint-reading course. A valuable skill I needed to brush up on. I also learned a healthy respect for my fellow students. These team members were bright people.

At the same time I was developing a real respect for my Division Managers. They too were bright, able people when given the chance. And wonder of wonders; as

I treated them better, they returned the favor! We were actually beginning to work together.

I was also discovering that the secrets to being Gung Ho yourself were the same as they were for organizations. After all, an organization is only as Gung Ho as the team members are. Andy and I may have talked about Gung Ho'ing the plant, but what we were really doing was getting individuals Gung Ho about their own work. And I was making progress with the Division Managers. Rather, they were making progress toward being Gung Ho themselves, and I was beginning to appreciate how talented they really were.

Establishing well-understood and shared goals was also progressing. But this too was going to take time. Andy's assessment was simple. "We're at chicken level involvement and we need pig commitment."

"What?"

"It's the old story of the barnyard breakfast," answered Andy. "The chicken and the pig agree to co-host and the chicken suggests they serve bacon and eggs. The pig replies, 'For you that means involvement. For me it's total commitment.' We need pig commitment."

Unfortunately, this level of commitment wasn't going to happen overnight. But, as Andy said, people were getting involved and we'd made a good start.

It was one thing to subscribe to the principles. Quite another to make them part of the life of the factory.

While everyone showed interest, there were two major stumbling blocks.

First, team members had to be willing, even eager, to take on considerable extra responsibility. People don't do that without time to think. Lots of time. Pig commitment is never instant, Andy told me.

Second, managers had to give up the levers of control they'd worked a lifetime to get hold of. They'd suffered fifteen years or more to get a lever to yank and now we were saying there was a better way: Don't yank the lever!

Besides, if they didn't yank team members' levers, what were they to do? Believing there was a meaningful management role beyond lever yanking required a stretch. Again, pig commitment wasn't going to come quickly.

I was pleased at the progress on value setting, but Andy soon set me straight on that as well. "Values agreed on aren't worth squat until they've been tested by both time and vigorous assault. You pass up doubling factory profit for three or four years in a row to uphold a value, then it's a value. Until then it's a nice idea."

But we were making progress. Friday I was sitting in my office thinking that all in all, it had been a pretty good week. I guess Old Man Morris was sitting in his office worried I might be thinking just that.

"Time to pull Peggy's chain," he must have thought. Why else tell me?

"Moved the year-end executive committee meeting up to December fifteenth. Just thought you'd like to know" was exactly what I heard after answering the phone. One thing about Morris. He sure knew how to play the power game. I was getting better at it myself.

"Great," I said. "We should be starting to show some brighter numbers by then. The end of December ones will look even better."

"I doubt it," he drawled.

Another thing about Old Man Morris. Always a ray of sunshine!

"We'll do our best, sir," I said brightly. All the time thinking, "Small-pie twit!"

I didn't care for the news, but I didn't feel as if I was being unfairly picked on. Old Man Morris had one or two buddies in the system, but he treated all of his plant managers about the same. He liked to keep his managers dangling from a mountain face on a frayed rope. While I might be about to lose my plant, others with good results would be up all night worried for their jobs if good didn't go to excellent by year end.

Andy arrived as I sat there, staring at the phone, thinking these deep philosophical thoughts.

"Ah, my Sherpa guide. Come on in."

"What?"

"Sorry. Just thinking about mountain climbing. What's up?"

"I was picking up the weekend computer run and thought I'd let you know Gift of the Goose is at hand. The weather is cooling up north and I expect tomorrow, right on schedule, we'll have Gift of the Goose."

"Hey! That's great, Andy. Just the tonic I need," and I told him of Morris's phone call.

"Good thing you didn't tell him we're counting on having until at least next summer to prove we can do it," said Andy. "It would have spoiled his weekend."

"And if we can't, it's 'heads held high,' right, Andy?"

"Sure thing. But don't forget I've got a plan. In the meantime, you'll be glad to know the motorcycle is put away and my half ton is back on the road. Pick you up seven A.M. tomorrow?"

"Sure thing," I said, mustering what enthusiasm I could for the early start. At least enclosed transportation was available for fall and winter. Although I'd miss the motorcycle.

When we rolled out of Walton on the dot of seven the next morning, Andy told me our destination was Hutchison Marsh, fifty-three miles away. A canoe hung over the back of the truck's box. A red bandanna fluttered from the stern. It was dark. It was cold. Overnight the temperature had dropped below freezing. In the cab Andy had a thermos of coffee and some doughnuts. I missed the motorcycle much less than I thought I might.

"I hear close to one hundred thousand geese have arrived in the last ten days. No trouble discovering Gift of the Goose, that's for sure."

"I'm ready, Andy."

I may have been ready, but I knew there wasn't any sense asking Andy anything until he decided the time was right. I had learned a lot from Andy, including patience.

Our conversation died. Andy must have been listening to the silence, waiting for it to end. Behind us, as we headed due west, the sun crept up over the horizon and lit the landscape with pinks, purples, and long morning shadows. In one field cattle leaving a shelter crossed a hill and were silhouetted against the sky. I may have been city born and bred, but I felt I was in the right place. I snuggled down into my jacket, hands around my warm mug of coffee, and wondered if I might be allowed to ride forever with Andy.

An hour later we passed a sign: HUTCHISON MARSH CONSERVATION AREA. NO HUNTING.

"No hunting. We'll be seeing lots of geese now," said Andy. "Soon as hunting season starts, those geese stick close to a game refuge."

"How do they know?" I wondered.

"Good question. Some hunters swear they can read the 'No Hunting' signs! All I know is that they are damn smart birds."

Sure enough, a mile down the road Andy pointed to a large V of geese. By the time we reached the edge of the marsh we'd spotted hundreds of geese. Minutes ago I'd thought I'd be content to ride forever, but now I was alert and eager to learn Grandfather's last secret: The Gift of the Goose.

Andy carried the canoe to the water, strapped me into a life jacket, and showed me how to climb into the canoe with the paddle across the gunnel for balance. From the back of the truck he fetched a gray canvas sack and, after securing his own life jacket, pushed off. The sun was now high in the cloudless morning sky.

I was glad to see there weren't any rapids around to test if we had a boat or a canoe. This vessel floated, and that was test enough for me.

From the stern Andy paddled the canoe swiftly into the marsh. Reeds parted and scraped along the side. Autumn-ripened seeds burst from bulrushes at our touch and floated away, leaving the brown crowns blotched with white scars. Wings flashed red as startled blackbirds flitted from reed to reed. As we moved farther into the marsh a cloud of mist hovered in the cool air over the warmer water.

Ahead the water grasses ended and we came upon an area of open water, a pond within a pond. It was quite irregular in shape, with the thinning and thickening of water plants along the edge making it difficult to determine just where the sides might be. Andy moved the canoe into the open water and began to set out goose decoys. They had been carved by Grandfather but without the fine detail.

The decoys set, Andy slipped the canoe back into the reeds. Through the tall grasses and bulrushes we could see the decoys, each anchored by a rope and small weight.

"Twenty years ago this marsh was gone. Drained dry. Then Ducks Unlimited came in and spent close to a million dollars restoring the wetland," Andy told me as he slid down into the bottom of the canoe and propped his head up on a life cushion wedged against his seat.

"Let me guess, Andy. You're going to have a rest. I'm going to watch geese. Right?"

"You got it," laughed Andy. "But this time your job is easy. Lots more geese than squirrels or beaver. And Gift of the Goose is all over the place. I expect we'll have some geese of our own soon. But no need to wait. As I said, Gift of the Goose is all over the place."

"It's here right now?" I questioned as a flock of honking geese flew high over head.

"Absolutely," laughed Andy. "The Gift of the Goose brings enthusiasm to Spirit of the Squirrel and Way of the Beaver."

Enthusiasm! Just the thought of adding enthusiasm to the Gung Ho process had me eagerly watching the geese. A large V flew over us much lower than the previous ones.

They must have spotted our decoys because they turned and flew back over us before continuing on.

"Why didn't they land? Don't they like Grandfather's decoys?" I teased Andy.

"Who knows? Maybe they're into plastic ones."

As if wishing to protest, the geese again turned and headed toward us. This time they came straight in. Wings flashed forward as brakes while flat webbed feet jutted out and down to touch the water. Split seconds before touching, the geese pulled in their wings, dropped with a splash onto the water, and came to an abrupt halt.

"Aren't they incredible? They really are huge," I said to Andy, then wondered if talking would frighten them away. The geese didn't seem too bothered, but when I moved to adjust the way I was sitting, I startled them. In a flash they were off. And as they rose up they all began to honk. A rock concert couldn't have been louder.

"What a noise," I said.

"They may be loud, but those geese have an important message for you. They go way beyond squirrels and beavers."

"There's more honking than a freeway in rush hour," I marveled.

"Gift of the Goose," said Andy. I should have guessed, but I didn't.

Andy gave me a second chance. "So, what's the honking all about? Who are the geese honking at?"

Suddenly I realized we weren't just having a pleasant conversation. We were zeroing in on Gift of the Goose. Who were the geese honking at?

"Each other?" I ventured.

"Correct. And why are they honking?"

I thought about this. I guessed they must be sending messages but by now I knew Andy well enough to know he'd reply, "What message?"

Squirrels chattered away to scold the world. Beavers whacked tails to send warning messages. In the next ten minutes several flocks of honking geese flew by. I concluded that unlike squirrels who seemed to chatter at anything and everything, these geese were definitely talking to each other. Further, their honking was so frequent they couldn't be sending warnings as beavers did. If it was a warning, something would change, but honking seemed to make no difference to flight patterns. They'd certainly honked their hearts out when they lifted off from our decoys, but they'd also honked as they landed.

I also noticed that from time to time the lead goose would fall back and the V would form up behind a new lead goose. But again, there didn't seem to be any connection to the honking.

"They must be honking a message, Andy. But it's not a warning and it's not tied into switching the lead."

"If it's not a warning, what's the opposite?"

I thought for a minute. "That everything is going well?"

"Even better. What's even better?"

"That everything is great? Fantastic? Terrific?"

"Of course," said Andy. "They are cheering each other on. Just listen to them."

I listened and Andy was right. They were honking encouragement and cheering each other. I'd been a cheerleader in high school and I knew a cheer when I heard one. These were enthusiastic, cheering honks.

"Here it is," said Andy, again reaching into the decoy sack. This time he unwrapped a detailed carving of a Canada goose. I quickly turned it over. There it was. The third secret that was to save Walton Works and likely the most valuable one of all:

—

The Gift of the Goose:
Cheering Others On

—

I sat there stunned by the Gift of the Goose. It was so simple. So obvious. So powerful. It was magnificent.

"Andy, if we start cheering people on. . . If we start giving encouragement. . . If we really get in there and do it—let people know how great they are. . ." I left the conclusion unspoken. There just didn't seem to be words big enough to describe what I wanted to say.

Andy knew exactly what I meant. "You're right. Spirit of the Squirrel and Way of the Beaver provide the spark. The Gift of the Goose is like throwing gasoline on the spark."

Then it hit me.

"Am I dense or just thick? When the Division Managers toured the finishing department your team member kept going on and on about all the wonderful things that happened. All the cheers. Everything from sales to birthdays and how you'd stop by and congratulate him on what he was doing. And I missed it. It was right there and I missed it."

"I wondered if you'd pick up on that," laughed Andy as he paddled back out for the decoys. "Good thing you didn't. It was too soon after learning the Way of the Beaver. When people discover the power of Gift of the Goose there is no stopping them. Grandfather's lessons may be simple, but they need time to settle in. You need to get some sparks going before you fan the flames with Gift of the Goose. Besides, out here you can learn directly from the geese. That's a lesson you'll never forget."

Overhead, on cue, geese came honking past.

"Those geese fly thousands of miles every year. They can move hundreds of miles in a day. They are truly one of the wonders of our world. And they do it cheering each other on every step of the way."

While Andy bagged the decoys I watched another V of geese and quickly made another discovery.

"Andy, all the geese honk. It isn't just the lead goose honking. They're all honking. It doesn't just have to be managers cheering the team members, does it? We can get everyone cheering each other."

"Of course," said Andy. "The Gift of the Goose is for everybody. Grandfather said:

—

The Gift of the Goose
Is God's Gift
We Give Each Other.

—

We slid through the reeds back to the edge of the marsh. As we pulled the canoe out of the water I could see black undulating V's of geese in every direction moving across the blue sky. Honking filled the air with joy. A gift they gave each other. It really must be God's gift, I decided. It was so wonderful.

"I can see why you said the Gift of the Goose brings enthusiasm to Spirit of the Squirrel and Way of the Beaver."

"It's how you make a mission come alive," said Andy as he lifted the canoe over the truck's tailgate. "People who set out to accomplish something that they believe is important and worthwhile—that's right work—need to make a contribution to the way that work is done—that's right way. Put those two together and you've got a mission. But the driving force behind people as they pursue a true mission is a reason for doing the work. A need to be fulfilled. You reward people by fulfilling those needs. Gung Ho people do right work, the right way, for the right reward. Grandfather used to say, 'No score, no game.'"

Andy pulled a couple of folding chairs from the back and set us up alongside the truck. "Canoes are great, but at my age a lawn chair is more comfortable for sitting in the sun."

"No score, no game?" I reminded Andy as I sat down.

"Sports teams must be about the most Gung Ho organizations you can name, but try to think about a basketball game where no one kept score and fans didn't cheer."

"Pretty bleak, all right."

"Darn tootin' it's bleak. Professional athletes would show up for the money, but it wouldn't be the same and that's important to understand. People are rewarded in two ways and both are important. Grandfather called them the two C's: cash and congratulations."

Then Andy told me something that rated a poster all of its own on my office wall.

"Einstein put it best:

$$E = mc^2$$

"Of course, Einstein was a bit mixed up about exactly what C squared meant. Obviously it means two C's. Enthusiasm equals mission times cash and congratulations."

"I like that," I said as I repeated the formula.

"So do I, and best of all, it works," replied Andy. "It reminds us that both cash and congratulations are important. But cash comes first. You have to feed a person's material needs, food and clothing, et cetera, before you can feed their spirit with congratulations."

"I like the idea of feeding the spirit. Will any congratulation do?"

"Good question. You need to be sure you're genuinely congratulating. Congratulations are simply an affirmation that who people are and what they do matter and that they are making a valuable contribution toward achieving the shared mission—right work done the right way. Spirit of the Squirrel. Way of the Beaver."

"What do I do if there just isn't anything to congratulate someone for?" I asked.

"Another good question. First, there's always *something*. You have to practice finding positive things though, and that's tough to do when you've spent your management career looking for things people do wrong."

"Am I that bad?" I asked, but Andy didn't answer my question right away.

"Second, when you can't outright congratulate some-one, you can always encourage them. And words of encouragement mean you have faith in their ability, and by acknowledging that ability you've also paid them a compliment. Congratulated them."

Then came my answer. I loved it!

"And no, you're not that bad. In fact you're really very good. Look at the fantastic job you've already done with Spirit of the Squirrel and Way of the Beaver. Your progress is nothing short of spectacular!"

Andy was right. Congratulations did feed the spirit. And boost enthusiasm. So much so, I had another question.

"Why are people so focused on cash rewards? That's all most people ever talk about. I've yet to see anyone go on strike for more congratulations."

"Sure you have," said Andy. "People just don't admit it. Lots of labor troubles have spirit issues at the core. Lack of respect may be the biggest. But you'd look a little silly walking around with a picket sign demanding affirmations that what you do matters and that your contribution is valuable. So cash becomes the measuring stick. It's easy to count and it's easy to compare."

Andy paused for a moment while we both watched a flock of geese pass overhead, honking encouragement to each other.

"Another thing," Andy continued. "Material needs are a base issue. We need food, clothes, and shelter to survive. Naturally money becomes a first concern, so we start by focusing on that and get so focused it's tough to move on.

"Management is as much to blame as team members. Any manager has only so much cash for payroll, and when it runs out, that's it. No personal responsibility. But every manager has an unlimited supply of congratulations available. If they come up short it's their own fault, and Longclaw's rule of management says managers abhor responsibility as nature does a vacuum."

"So focusing on cash suits both team members and management," I said. "Team members have an easy way to measure and compare themselves to others, and managers don't have to feel responsible if they can't deliver everything the team members would like."

"We're falling into the same trap," Andy said. "Here we are talking about cash, the easy C, when we should be paying attention to the other C, congratulations. Remember I said congratulations were affirmations? Well, there are both active and passive affirmations and Walton Works #2 won't be Gung Ho without both. Active affirmations are the kind you usually think of. Telling people what a great job they've done or presenting an award. Passive affirmations can be even more powerful.

"A classic example would be sitting on your hands, biting your tongue, and looking unconcerned and confident as one of your team members carries forward a tricky, complicated, and important project. Just the kind of project you excel at, and every fiber of your body is crying out to take control—or at least issue a couple of warnings about potential trouble spots. But you don't. And your silence sends a very clear message to the worker: 'You're good. You can handle this. I trust you.'

"Perhaps for those geese up there, honking encouragement and praise may be the best they can do, but for people it's often passive affirmations that are the most important. Rah-rah awards banquets may or may not be B.S. Giving somebody the tools to do the job and then, provided they are competent, getting out of their way is always real."

It was about the longest speech I had ever heard Andy give on anything. I knew what he'd said was important, and so I gave it some space of its own before going on.

Eventually, after a period of silence, I said, "You say that sometimes rah-rah isn't real. Isn't that a problem?

I mean, if you're constantly congratulating people, doesn't it become false?"

"Not as long as it's true congratulations, it doesn't," said Andy. "Something else I learned from Grandfather: true congratulations. First of all, true obviously means genuine. Then true stands for:

> *T imely*
> *R esponsive*
> *U nconditional*
> *E nthusiastic*

"You can't overdo congratulations if they are true congratulations. And congratulations, active and passive, are powerful stuff. So powerful in fact that some managers think they can get away with substituting them for cash. And to a certain extent you can. The military are masters at it. Gold braid on the hat and a chest full of tin and young people volunteer to get shot at despite a thin pay packet!"

Andy shook his head in wonder.

"Unfortunately, or perhaps fortunately, it isn't so easy in most organizations," he continued. "First and foremost you have to pay people fairly. But once you do, you'll be a lot further ahead heaping on the congratulations and feeding the soul rather than just loading on more cash."

"I'm sure I will be," I replied. "Gift of the Goose is going to make more of a difference than Spirit of the Squirrel or Way of the Beaver did, I bet."

"Only because they're already going. The Gift of the Goose doesn't have the impact unless the Spirit of the Squirrel and Way of the Beaver are also present. Otherwise it would be like spreading fertilizer on rock. A few fast sprouts where a little seed and soil meet in a crevice perhaps, but nothing worthwhile or permanent."

We sat enjoying the sun and listening to the geese for a long time. Then either the silence ended, or Andy's lunch alarm sounded the alert. "Time to feed material needs. How about brunch at that café we passed just outside the marsh area?"

As we ate, Andy gave me two guidelines. The first he had me write down on a pad of paper he'd pulled from the glove compartment:

Programmed	→	Spontaneous
Blanket	→	Individual
General	→	Specific
Traditional	→	Unique

Andy said congratulations could be placed on a continuum from left to right. The further to the right congratulations were, the more effective they were. Spontaneous, individual, specific, and unique congratulations were always better than programmed, blanket, general, and traditional ones.

"An annual message to the whole department congratulating them on a good year by way of a memo pinned on the bulletin board won't have the impact of an announcement on the paging system that Leslie Anderson in Shipping has set a record for cartons shipped without damage three months in a row."

The second guideline was to cheer the progress, not just the result. "At a football game the crowd doesn't sit mute in the stands while the home team moves the ball to first down and goal to go and then cheer only when the touchdown comes. But that's what most organizations do. Worse, they score in November and then wait until the annual award dinner in February, a hundred or so games later, to cheer."

The more I heard, the more I became convinced the Gift of the Goose was the way to cook Old Man Morris's goose, if only we had enough time.

As soon as we were back in Walton I headed for the plant. Once our furnaces were fired up, we kept the run going, and I knew we had a full crew in over the weekend. A full crew of great people doing great things and I needed to get down to the factory and tell them.

I had a ball! As I toured the shop floor and gave the gift God gave us to give each other, amazing things began to happen. When I honked true congratulations, team members began honking back.

"Good to see you here."

"Thanks for that."

"Miss Sinclair, you're doing a great job. We're all behind you. And that's the first time anyone's said that to a General Manager, I can tell you."

I'd gone in to bolster them and they were bolstering me!

I felt like a traitor though. These people were really beginning to edge into Gung Ho but we didn't have the time to pull it off. They were responding to the Spirit of the Squirrel, the Way of the Beaver, and now the Gift of the Goose, but I knew Old Man Morris's response was going to be layoff notices for all of them.

I called Andy at home Sunday evening. "I've been down at the plant working on Gift of the Goose and we can do it, Andy. That whole place will go Gung Ho. I can feel it in my bones. But we're toying with them, Andy. You and I may think we're going out with our heads held high, but I think perhaps they should be bowed in shame. We're just playing with their lives. We don't have the time."

"I have a plan," Andy replied simply. "By this time next week I hope it will be working. And if not, it's still heads held high. The only hope that plant's got is Gung Ho."

Then Andy gave me a healthy dose of encouragement. We had no concrete results to cheer, but he was most complimentary about how I'd done so far and I knew he meant it.

Monday morning, my spirits much improved, I made my poster. The message was fantastic. My goose was magnificent.

GIFT OF THE GOOSE:
CHEERING OTHERS ON

1. Active or passive, congratulations must be TRUE.

2. No score, no game, and cheer the progress.

3. $E = mc^2$—Enthusiasm equals mission times cash and congratulations.

Wednesday Andy dropped his bombshell.

That day's *Walton Weekly Advertiser* covered the story on its front page. Timothy "Longhorn" Anderson, the son of our founder and our current Chairman of the Board, was to be awarded the first ever Walton Medal of Honor.

The story quoted Longhorn as being delighted with the award. So pleased, in fact, he'd pledged $25,000 of company money to help cover expenses.

The award ceremony, complete with parade and brass bands invited from ten surrounding towns, would be held the following July 4. Andy Longclaw, of the Workers' Council, and Walton's Mayor, Samuel P. Johnston, had made the announcement!

A phone call from the Mayor was the first I heard of the story. He was, he said, pleased to be included in the ceremony, but it was embarrassing not to know anything about it until he read it in the paper. The city would be glad to co-sponsor the award, he assured me, but it would have been nice to be consulted. My thoughts exactly.

I placed the next call to Andy. "I didn't know we had a Workers' Council."

"Brand-new this morning," said Andy.

"And what's this about the Mayor not knowing? He's been on the phone to me."

"You think he's surprised? You should have heard Longhorn when I called him a few minutes ago," laughed Andy. "He didn't mind being quoted as being pleased, but he sure was surprised about the $25,000 when I read him that part."

"You called him? You called Longhorn?"

"Sure thing. Met him when he worked here. He's been coming up to hunt with me every fall for fifteen years. There's got to be some advantages to being an Indian, you know. Everyone who isn't an Indian thinks we know where the deer are. Anyway, I always call about this time of year to set up hunting, and so when the story appeared, I figured the least I could do was call and congratulate him."

"He didn't know about it? Or the $25,000?"

"Na, I figured I'd do the story first, then tell him. I knew he'd be good for the cash."

"You wrote the story?" I choked out. "You made it all up?"

"Not all of it. The part about inviting the brass bands was true. I did call them," Andy said defensively.

I had no possible reply and let the silence hang.

"It's ancient native wisdom," Andy assured me.

"Grandfather, I suppose."

"Grandmother, actually. She said she could get Grandfather to do anything she wanted by announcing it and thanking him with lavish praise in public. Grandfather loved to play the part and so do Longhorn and the Mayor."

"Your grandmother was a traitor to all women, telling you that. Those tricks are privileged information men are not supposed to know anything about," I declared firmly.

Then it hit me. Suddenly I understood what this was all about.

"Andy," I cried out. "It's our year, isn't it? You've set this up eight months out. Longhorn gets his big award next July. Old Man Morris won't dare touch us, unless we really go into the tank, until next July."

"That's the way I figure it. One thing I've learned about Longhorn in fifteen years is he does like to be fussed over, he does like to shoot the biggest deer, and I happen to know he loves parades. I think it would be worth Old Man Morris's job to mess with this plant before next July fourth. Only one problem though."

"What's that?"

"Come July fifth we could be toast. The only thing Longhorn likes better than glory is money, and if we're still costing him money come July fifth, he'll close us as easily as you and I do a door."

"May I ask a question, Andy?"

"Shoot."

"How did you get this in the paper?"

"Easy. The owner, who is also the editor, doesn't like writing much. He worked with me in the plant until his dad died and he took over the paper. I've been writing his lead editorial for years. It's fun. And he's always willing to run stories I do. Up to now it's mostly been gags on birthdays. But he was sure happy to have the scoop on the Longhorn award."

Andy had done it! We had our year. Provided, of course, we didn't mess up too badly in the meantime. Given our problems and the possible pitfalls ahead, calling the ten months from September to July a year, and feeling we really had a year, didn't seem like that big a deal.

Longhorn was thrilled with his award. His father had always been the one to garner all the awards and attention. This was Longhorn's first debut in the spotlight for himself—not representing the company or his father, but for himself—and it proved to be a heady drug indeed.

At the time I was excited to think we could save the plant. Later I wondered if it wasn't wrong to have tricked Longhorn. Andy's response was clear.

"I'm not proud of taking advantage of Longhorn's character flaws," he said, "but I'm damn proud to have helped save fifteen hundred jobs. I've got no problem with creating a plan to divert Longhorn's attention to give us a chance. The real problem would be looking those people and their kids in the face if I didn't!" Andy, as always, put issues into perspective, and as he did so I found myself totally in agreement.

Thankfully Old Man Morris didn't scent the setup. I don't think he figured I'd be smart enough to do it. And I guess he was right. He just didn't know about Andy!

Besides, Longhorn had several connections with the plant in addition to hunting. The award wasn't quite as surprising to head office as it might otherwise have seemed.

Longhorn worked in the plant one summer when he was at college and had spent a year as assistant plant manager at Walton, which was how he'd got tied up with Andy in the first place.

Even his nickname, Longhorn, traced back to his time at Walton. He'd placed a Longhorn steer in the General Manager's office one night. The GM had the habit of telling young Mr. Anderson all his ideas were B.S. By the morning the steer had left a pile or two of the real stuff for the GM to contemplate, and young Mr. Anderson was on hand to point out the difference between the real thing and his ideas to the GM. From that day on he was known as Longhorn. A name he apparently treasured. There are advantages to your family's owning the company that they never tell you about in business school.

"Longhorn's still as arrogant. Only more polished," Andy observed. "Some folks are born with a silver spoon in their mouths and lick it for the rest of their lives. Some spit it out. Longhorn's one of those who swallowed it whole."

Thank heavens he did. Old Man Morris kept blustering. But after Longhorn's hunting trip, followed by a visit to the Mayor's office and a dinner with the hastily assembled Workers' Council, complete with toasts, cheers, and not a mention of Longhorn's father, Old Man Morris's blustering was much muted.

By February our numbers had turned. At the April Board meeting I heard Old Man Morris was taking full credit for the wisdom in appointing "that Sinclair gal" to run the plant. Our first-half results were so good we were on a par with average plant results in our whole system.

I now realize that high school physics texts are excellent management primers. Bodies at rest have inertia. It requires extra energy to get them moving, but once going they have momentum. If Andy's three secrets were stones, I imagine each would be a different size for everyone, and for every organization. Some would be harder to move than others—but once they were on the move, watch out!

Once we set the fire of Worthwhile Work burning, the first secret kept rolling. From time to time we had to push and pull, but the first secret developed a momentum of its own. So did the third secret: Cheering Each Other On. The toughest part was Andy's second secret: people being in Control of Achieving the Goal.

Managers had to be convinced that coaching—which we defined as teaching and practice focused on taking action, with celebration when things go well and supportive redirection when things go wrong, while all the time creating excitement and challenge for those being coached—would produce better results than hard, unforgiving, demanding control.

While the organization's biggest challenge was the second secret, mine was the third: Cheering Each Other On. I'd spent my career at head office. That meant being a policeman—catching rule breakers and hauling in the guilty for punishment. I certainly wasn't a natural when it came to seeking out the best people for cheers, or encouraging the worst people and praising them when they did something right.

Success, I've decided, is all about attitude, energy, balance, and connecting with others. Best of all, once you get a taste of it, you start to spread it around. Like love, the more you give, the more you get. Today I try to spread sunshine wherever I go. It's more productive and more fun than my former role of policeman of the world.

How did it happen? How did people change? It was just like Andy said. Trust. Telling the truth. Building self-esteem. Rewarding people who didn't yank levers. Rewarding those who shared information. Setting stretching goals. Living our values. Training, training, training, and then more training. And not just on plant-related topics. A learning, growing mind is an open mind, and we needed open minds.

Then cheering. Lots and lots of cheering. We challenged everyone in the plant to catch other people doing something right. And when they did, they called Gung Ho Central.

The single most important productivity tool in our whole plant is kept at Gung Ho Central. It's a Polaroid camera. The minute they receive a report of a team member doing something right, the people at Gung Ho Central rush to the scene of the incident, with Polaroid camera in hand, to catch the perpetrator in action.

Color copies are quickly posted throughout the plant. The police put up Wanted posters; we put up Caught posters. And under the team member's picture we clearly state exactly what we caught him or her doing.

That's essentially how we did it, and do it now—and you can too. The principles are the same no matter what your organization: sales, insurance, retail, brokerage, restaurant, doctor's office, or government department. The secrets of the squirrel, beaver, and goose will work for your organization and they'll work for you personally as well. It takes time though. There's no sense starting out unless you're willing to stick with it. Gung Ho is not a quick fix. Not flavor of the week, month, or even year. It's flavor of the five-year strategic planning cycle. It's a way of life. Like most things that are hard fought for, though, it's well worth the wait. Both for team members and the organization.

I said one of the ingredients of success was energy. Enthusiasm is positive energy. I have come to believe that human minds, when linked to a common purpose, are like a series of linked computers. Together they achieve infinitely more than they would acting alone. And when it comes to enthusiasm, the mind is again similar to a computer. I can program my computer to be a word processor or an analyzer of engineering designs. I can program my brain to be unhappy with every eventuality, or to look forward enthusiastically to the day ahead. I choose to be enthusiastic. I choose to be Gung Ho. I live a Gung Ho life.

If you want to be Gung Ho, don't just decide to be Gung Ho. Constantly, deliberately, and systematically live a Gung Ho life. And if you're going to Gung Ho an organization, you better be sure your agent of change lives a Gung Ho life too. You wouldn't hire a drunk to teach your children to drive. Don't put a small-pie grump in charge of Gung Ho.

The knowledge of what to do to be Gung Ho is important, of course. But what really counts is doing it. Taking action. Now. Today.

It took us the full three years to reach a level Andy was willing to certify as Gung Ho and several more before we attracted national attention and found ourselves in the White House Rose Garden.

I won't pretend it was all easy or that we didn't backslide as part of moving forward. But it was fun.

Andy enjoyed Gung Ho'ing the plant as well. Matter of fact, after Andy's first heart attack I discovered he was a diabetic and got after him for not taking better care of himself. "Lady," he said with a smile, "if I'd known you'd be along and we'd have this much fun Gung Ho'ing Walton Works #2, I'd have done just that."

The best part was the whole plant enjoyed our success. Profit-sharing bonuses looked after cash needs, and everybody heaped as many active and passive congratulations on each other as they could.

I loved beating Old Man Morris. I was thrilled to meet the President. But my greatest joy is to go down to the gate at shift change and watch the team members walk out the very gate where it all began on Andy's motorcycle so long ago. Today all the team members go home with their heads held high. They're doing important work, each has significant input into how to do it, and they know that both the company and their fellow workers appreciate their efforts and success.

The Spirit of the Squirrel.

The Way of the Beaver.

The Gift of the Goose.

Gung Ho!

AFTERWORD

by Peggy Sinclair

When I first agreed to do this project with Ken and Sheldon, the only thing I asked for was the right to put my own words at the end. I thought there might be something I needed to say. I had faith in Ken and Sheldon, but my commitment to Andy dictated I keep this last bit of control to ensure the story was properly told. And the story has been properly told. There's not a word I'd change. I thank Ken and Sheldon for that and for suggesting dedicating this book to Andy and his family, Jean and Robert. For that I'll be forever grateful.

I'm also grateful to the team at Walton Works #2. You all know who you are. Gung Ho!

Obviously our plant name has been changed. After the White House award we all learned to value our privacy.

But equally important, this isn't our story. It isn't even Andy's story or Grandfather's. It is and can be the story of every organization in our great country, be it a business, a school, a hospital, or a government department, that chooses to be Gung Ho.

If I may be permitted, I'll close with a personal word.

After Andy's first heart attack, I moved him out of the finishing department and made him Assistant General Manager with an office next to mine. He wasn't happy to leave his team, but I told him it was the ultimate passive congratulation he could give. Between that and his doctor's ordering him off the floor, he grudgingly agreed. Just before his last illness he began to talk about the need to teach Gung Ho to the rest of the world. I'm honored to have had a small role in perpetuating his legacy.

The day of his funeral we closed the plant, and I think every able-bodied man, woman, and child over sixteen in town was at the service. As was Longhorn. Old Man Morris wasn't there. He'd left the company shortly after our early success under some sort of cloud. We were never sure what it was and we didn't care.

Not long after the funeral I had a call from a lawyer. Andy had one final surprise and gift for me. Most of his estate, which thanks to Grandfather's carvings and Andy's frugal lifestyle was substantial, was left to a local children's agency in memory of his son. I was left his cabin. The cabin and my memories have made it easy to turn down offers of heading up a larger plant and even a senior position at head office.

I write sitting on the porch. The skunks are long gone, but I'll go down to feed Andy's squirrels, birds, and rabbits when I'm finished. In the shed is the motorcycle. Sometimes I go out, climb on the back, close my eyes, and soon I'm whipping down the highway, clinging to the back of my best friend.

Gung Ho, Andy.

Gung Ho, friend.

GUNG HO
GAME PLAN

As Peggy and Andy worked to Gung Ho Walton Works #2, they developed a game plan chart which was posted in every office, in the cafeteria, and throughout the plant. To assist readers wishing to become Gung Ho themselves or to Gung Ho an organization, we are pleased, with Peggy's permission, to reproduce this poster and the reassessment guides. On the original posters, the reassessment guideposts were printed under the game plan. Here you'll find them on the pages following the game plan.

GUNG HO GAME PLAN

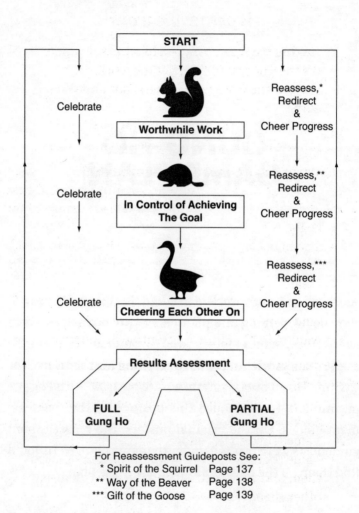

For Reassessment Guideposts See:
* Spirit of the Squirrel   Page 137
** Way of the Beaver   Page 138
*** Gift of the Goose   Page 139

REASSESSMENT GUIDEPOST I
THE SPIRIT OF THE SQUIRREL

Worthwhile work

1. **Knowing we make the world a better place.**
   - It's the understanding, not the work.
   - It's how the work helps others, not units dealt with.
   - Result: self-esteem—an emotion whose power ranks right up there with love and hate.

2. **Everyone works toward a shared goal.**
   - Goal sharing means buy-in, not announcing. Trust and putting team members first lead to support for goals.
   - The manager sets critical goals. The team can set the rest. (People support best that which they help create.)
   - Goals are marker posts you drive into the future landscape between where you are and where you want to be. They focus attention productively.

3. **Values guide all plans, decisions and actions.**
   - Goals are for the future. Values are now. Goals are set. Values are lived. Goals change. Values are rocks you can count on. Goals get people going. Values sustain the effort.
   - Values become real only when you demonstrate them in the way you act and the way you insist others behave.
   - In a Gung Ho organization, values are the real boss.

REASSESSMENT GUIDEPOST II
THE WAY OF THE BEAVER

In control of achieving the goal

1. **A playing field with clearly marked territory.**
   - Goals and values define the playing field and rules of the game.
   - Leaders decide what position team members play but then have to get off the field and let the players move the ball.
   - Freedom to take charge comes from knowing exactly what territory is yours.

2. **Thoughts, feelings, needs, and dreams are respected, listened to, and acted upon.**
   - You can't be in control unless the rest of the organization supports you and doesn't rip you, or your work, apart.
   - Golden Rule of Management: Value individuals as persons.
   - Information is the gatekeeper to power. Everybody needs full open access to information. Managers must be willing to give up the levers of control they've worked a lifetime to get hold of. It's tough to be boss without being bossy.

3. **Able but challenged.**
   - Production expectations should be within capacity and skills, but if you undershoot you'll insult.
   - Nothing drains self-esteem faster than knowing you're ripping off the system, not contributing.

If people can't do a fair day's work for a fair day's pay, you demean them.

- Gung Ho requires a stretch: work that demands people's best and allows them to learn and move ahead into uncharted territory.

REASSESSMENT GUIDEPOST III
THE GIFT OF THE GOOSE

Cheering each other on

1. **Active or passive, congratulations must be TRUE.**
   - Congratulations are affirmations that who people are and what they do matter, and that they are making a valuable contribution toward achieving the shared mission.
   - Telling people what a great job they've done or presenting an award is an active congratulation. Passive congratulations are such things as stepping aside and letting a team member go forward with a tricky, complicated, and important project, without exercising some sort of control or even offering advice.
   - You can't overdo TRUE congratulations: Timely, Responsive, Unconditional, Enthusiastic.

2. **No score, no game, and cheer the progress.**
   - At football games fans don't sit mute as the ball is moved down the field, waiting for the touchdown before cheering. Cheer the progress, not just

the results. Measurement (score) shared with everyone generates excitement.

- The farther congratulations are to the right on the scale below, the better (more effective) they are:

Programmed	→	Spontaneous
Blanket	→	Individual
General	→	Specific
Traditional	→	Unique

- Stop focusing on problems and the guilty party (police behavior) and start looking for those responsible for things gone right (coach behavior).

3. $E = mc^2$—**Enthusiasm equals mission times cash and congratulations.**
   - Worthwhile work and being in control of achieving the goal—that's a mission.
   - Cheering each other on brings enthusiasm to work.
   - Cash comes first—you need to feed material needs, (food, clothing, etc.) before you can feed the spirit with congratulations.

GOOSE HONKINGS

Ken and Sheldon are Raving Fans of...

Jake Beard, Willie Sather, and **John Peterson,** of Dean Witter Reynolds Inc. These "Three Wise Men of Wayzata" embody the spirit, warmth, generosity, and caring that mark the essence of a Gung Ho life. Their support, friendship, and wisdom have guided *Gung Ho!* from rough-draft manuscript to final book.

Sandra Ford, of the Sandra Ford Agency. Sandra's enthusiasm, hard work, and excellent advice are always appreciated.

Derek Johannson, of Carlyle Computer Products, whose perceptive comments have helped make this a better book and whose Gung Ho approach to life and business can serve as a model to all.

Senator Douglas D. Everett, of Royal Canadian Securities Limited, who for nearly thirty years has, for Sheldon, at various times been boss, partner, mentor, and always friend and valued adviser.

Our **Avis Rent-A-Car** gang of Gung Ho guides who have given wonderful advice: John Delano and Luke Medley from "down under" and the North American team of Bill Boxberger, Tom Byrnes, Robert Cardillo, Mike Caron, Michael Collins, Ross O'Donnell, John Forsythe, Sylvia Fried, John Gallager, Eddie Hassell, Russ James, Duncan Rhodes, Bob Salerno, Eric Schnitzler, John Sellers, and Pat Siniscalchi.

Pam La Palme of Scotiabank, who gave generously of her time in the midst of a mind-boggling busy schedule. Her hit-the-nail-on-the-head comments made us think and revise, and *Gung Ho!* is better for it.

Larry Hughes of Morrow has again provided patient, nurturing support. When we were stuck, or in doubt, "Ask Larry" has been our rallying cry. It worked every time!

Zach Schisgal and **Will Schwalbe** have been our editors at Morrow and deserve special thanks for their help. Two class guys who have helped make writing fun.

Margret McBride, Winifred Golden, Kim Sauer, and **Mindy Riesenberg** of the Margret McBride Agency. As literary agents it is their job to whip the manuscript into presentable form and represent our interests in dealings with the publisher. From editing to book cover design to explaining (for the umpteenth time) how foreign rights are covered in the publishing contract, they have nudged, massaged, pushed, and, when needed, given us a mighty whack to help the message sink in. In short, they are talented agents and treasured friends.

Bob Nelson, who was a key adviser when we wrote *Raving Fans!* and who today is a bestselling business author, following the phenomenal success of his *1001 Ways to Reward Employees*. Now *1001 Ways to Energize Employees* is on its way to similar success. We're mighty proud of you, Bob!

Ian and Sandy McLandress, Ted and Carolyn Ransby, Richard and Hillaine Kroft, Harvey and Sandra Secter, and **Sol Kanee** are special supportive people and each merits our sincere thanks.

The Baillie Lumber group has provided a fine example of Raving Fan Service® to customers with a Gung Ho team. In particular we thank Jeff Meyer, Don Meyer, George Thomson, and especially Jim McCauley, who opened the door.

At **Tenneco Automotive,** Tom Evans, Steve Strom, Barbara Posner, and Paul Johnson all gave thoughtful comments from a unique perspective. We give them our warmest thanks.

In Europe the **Standox** people at **Herberts GmbH** have been strong supporters of *Raving Fans!* and several have given us valuable feedback on *Gung Ho!* We thank

Dr. Jürgen Ritz, Rolf Janson, Herbert Born, and Werner Ranft in Germany and Bill Kregel and Mike Cash in America.

John Fulkerson, Vice President of Organization Capability, Kmart Corporation, and **Gina Ventre,** Vice President of Technical Support at Stop & Shop Companies, have been enthusiastic in their support for *Gung Ho!* Ken thanks them for their energy and Gung Ho spirit.

Frank Felicella of Builders Square, **Bob Kozminski** of Keystone Ford Sales, **Susan Goldie** of OnLine Business Systems, **Roger Emery** of Canadian Tire, **Jim Dickson** of Alcan Rolled Products, **Kerry Hawkins** of Cargill Limited, **Don Carr** of MTS Com, **Kristjan Backman** of Phoenix Recycling, **Dave Watson** of Precision Metalcraft, **Stuart Murray** of Domo Gas, Sandy Riley of Investors Group, **Hugh Goldie** of The Robert Thompson Partnership, and **Janet Smith**, Principal of The Canadian Centre for Management Development, have generously given of their time and talent. All brought a wealth of practical solid business experience to their advice and they will recognize the significant contribution they've made when they read *Gung Ho!*

Our work together has benefited from the support of **Richard Andison, Sheldon Berney, Trevor Cochrane, Carl Eisbrenner, Ray Kives, Mel Lazareck, Sam Linhart, Bob May, Michael Nozick, Maureen**

Prendiville, **Hartley Richardson, Ross Robinson, Gary Steiman,** and **Jim Tennant.** We thank them.

The two teams of support at Ken's and Sheldon's offices, led by **Eleanor Terndrup, Dana Kyle, Dee Kelly, Dorothy Morris, Bill McWilliams,** and **Rita Loewen.** As well, our special thanks to two talented men: **Harry Paul,** otherwise known as Mr. Make It Happen, and **Peter Psichogios,** for their wise counsel.

We also extend our thanks to **Anne Cole, Rebecca Goodhart, Patricia Ford, Susan Skinner, Maxime Worcester, Tom Arnett, Maryann Nevile, Frances Bowles, Jamie Hutchison, Carl M. Jenkins, Jr., Martin Strauss, Jack** and **Belva London, Lyle** and **Anna Silverman, Jim** and **Judy Fields, Paul and Carol Hill, John** and **Maureen Bracken, Eddie** and **Marsha Cowan, Jeff Golfman, Gordon Wiebe, Henrietta Wilde, Gaylene Chesnut, Ann Deluce, Bert Guinee, Matt Kaufmann, Paul Petrick, Phil Purcell, Richard DeMartini, James Higgins, Mitch Merin, Tom Schneider, Christine Edwards, Charles Fiumefreddo, Bob Dwyer, Bob Scanlan, Joe McAlinden, John Van Heuvelen, Jack Kemp, Bill McMahon, Robert Zimmerman, Doug Brown, Nancy Kennedy, Kathy Comerford, Christine Moss, David Lavin, Kathy Worrel, Richard Kelly, Jock Tooley, Claudette Griffin, Don Newman, Jack Thompson, Laurie Bremner, Mark Mancini, Don Tykeson, Dan**

Stevens, Mark Kinzel, Ian Thow, Richard Snell, Jim Babcock, Bill Jones, Dick Dawson, David Friesen, Michelle McPeek, Chuck Paton, Arnie Thorsteinson, Hubert Saint-Onge, Sam Katz, David Johnston, Ed Chornous, Hugo Sorensen, Paul Loewen, Tony Guertin, Jr., Danny Hooper, Bill Fast, Glen Sytnyk, Steve Schwartz, Bruce Hanson, Ted Chivers, Ron Hannon, John Wilson, and the talented writer Joan Rusen.

Wayne Dyer, Max DePree, Bob Galvin, Paul Hersey, Spencer Johnson, Harvey Mackay, Michael O'Connor, Tom Peters, Tony Robbins, Betsy Sanders, and Carl Sewell, all excellent authors, whose books have been an inspiration to us and millions of others.

One of the special joys of passing fifty is the opportunity to be joined by children in business. We feel particularly lucky to welcome Scott and Debbie Blanchard and Kingsley and Patti Bowles into our business lives. May they enjoy work and be Gung Ho in all they do.

We acknowledge our debt to our wives, Marjorie Blanchard and Penny Bowles. Whatever success we have enjoyed, or may find in the future, rests on their unfailing support in tough times and their challenge to continually improve in good times. Both are part of our business lives and have made important contributions to *Raving Fans!* and now *Gung Ho!* They are the wind beneath our wings.

Finally, we extend our warm and humble thanks to Peggy Sinclair. We acknowledge our debt in being allowed to tell the Gung Ho story. We too are honored to have had a role in perpetuating the legacy of Andy and his grandfather. Our regret at not having had the opportunity to meet Andy is mirrored by readers of the manuscript (and now, no doubt, the book) who want to find and meet Peggy. They ask if Peggy's name has been changed. They even ask if Andy was a real person. These questions will remain forever unanswered because, as Peggy has taught us, they are the wrong questions. John Donne said, ". . . never send to know for whom the bell tolls; it tolls for thee." The question each of us must face is, will the Gung Ho bell toll for us? Not, for whom does the bell now toll? If you're Gung Ho, then nothing could be more real and the identity of Peggy and Andy matters not. If you aren't, then it matters not either.

Gung Ho, Friend?

ABOUT THE AUTHORS

Ken Blanchard's impact as a writer in the field of management has been especially far-reaching. The bestselling business book of all time, *The One Minute Manager*® (1982), co-authored with Spencer Johnson, has sold over nine million copies and has been translated into more than twenty-five languages. Throughout 1996 *The One Minute Manager*® appeared on the Business Week Bestseller List along with three of Ken's most recent books, *Raving Fans!: A Revolutionary Approach to Customer Service* (1993), co-authored with entrepreneur Sheldon Bowles; *Everyone's a Coach* (1995), co-authored with National Football League legendary coach Don

Shula; and *Empowerment Takes More Than a Minute* (1995), co-authored with consulting partners John Carlos and Alan Randolph. No other author has had four books on this prestigious bestselling list in a single year.

Blanchard is chairman of Blanchard Training and Development, Inc., a full-service management consulting and training company that he co-founded in 1979 with his wife, Marjorie. The Blanchards are proud of the fact that their daughter, Debbie, and son, Scott, are also active in their business. Ken is also a visiting lecturer at his alma mater, Cornell University, where he is a Trustee Emeritus.

The Blanchards live in San Diego.

Sheldon Bowles is a successful entrepreneur, *New York Times* and *Business Week* bestselling author, and noted speaker. He began his career as a newspaper reporter, became vice president of Royal Canadian Securities, and then president and CEO of Domo Gas. With partner Senator Douglas Everett, he built that company into one of Canada's largest retail gasoline chains. At a time when competitors were going self-serve, Domo swept to success featuring "Jump to the Pump"® service with Gung Ho employees.

After leaving Domo, Sheldon, with three partners, turned a small manufacturing plant into a multimillion-dollar business. Sheldon now shares his hard-won knowledge of what works and what doesn't with audiences around the world and in his books, *Raving Fans!* and now *Gung Ho!*, both co-authored with Ken Blanchard.

Sheldon has been called "a customer service legend" by Harvey Mackay; "a master motivator of employees" by Bob Nelson; and "a stimulating and entertaining speaker with great take-home value" by Ken Blanchard. Audiences find him thought-provoking, inspirational, and fun; business colleagues describe him as having a passion for win-win thinking, action, and success; and friends testify to his ability to pluck humor and a lesson of life out of any situation.

Sheldon, wife, Penny, and children, Kingsley and Patti, live in Winnipeg.

SERVICES AVAILABLE

The Ken Blanchard Companies® is a global leader in workplace learning, productivity, performance, and leadership effectiveness that is best known for its Situational Leadership® II program—the most widely taught leadership model in the world. Because of its ability to help people excel as self-leaders and as leaders of others, SL II® is embraced by Fortune 500 companies as well as mid- to small-size businesses, governments, and educational and non-profit organizations.

Blanchard® programs, which are based on the evidence that people are the key to accomplishing strategic objectives and driving business results, develop excellence in leadership, teams, customer loyalty, change manage-ment, and performance improvement. The company's continual research points to best practices for workplace improvement, while its world-class trainers and coaches drive organizational and behavioral change at all levels and help people make the shift from learning to doing.

Leadership experts from The Ken Blanchard Companies are available for workshops, consulting, as well as keynote addresses on visioning, organizational devel-opment, workplace performance, and business trends.

Tools for Change

Visit kenblanchard.com and click on "Tools for Change" to learn about workshops, coaching services, and leader-ship programs that help your organization create lasting behavior changes that have a measurable impact.

Global Headquarters	**Europe, Middle-East, Africa**
The Ken Blanchard Companies	The Ken Blanchard Companies
125 State Place	Gateway Guildford, Power Close
Escondido CA 92029	
USA	Guildford, Surrey GU1 1EJ
	United Kingdom
1.800.728.6000 from United States	+44 (0) 1483 456300
1.760.489.5005 from outside the U.S.	Email: uk@kenblanchard.com
www.kenblanchard.com	www.kenblanchard.com

SOCIAL NETWORKING

Visit Blanchard on YouTube

Watch thought leaders from The Ken Blanchard Companies in action. Link and subscribe to Blanchard's channel, and you'll receive updates as new videos are posted. Visit www.youtube.com/KenBlanchardCos

Join the Blanchard Fan Club on Facebook

Be part of our inner circle and link to Ken Blanchard at Facebook. Meet other fans of Ken and his books. Access videos and photos, and get invited to special events. Visit www.facebook.com/KenBlanchardFanPage

Join Conversations with Ken Blanchard

Ken's blog, HowWeLead.org, was created to inspire positive change. It is a public service site devoted to leadership
topics that connect us all. It is a social network, where
you will meet people who care deeply about responsible
leadership. And it's a place where Ken Blanchard would
like to hear your opinion.

Ken's Twitter Updates

Receive timely messages and thoughts from Ken. Find
out the events he's attending and what's on his mind
@kenblanchard.